CW00820552

BROKEN THREADS

BROKEN THREADS

THE DESTRUCTION OF THE JEWISH FASHION
INDUSTRY IN GERMANY AND AUSTRIA

EDITED BY ROBERTA S. KREMER

BERG

Oxford · New York

VANCOUVER HOLOCAUST EDUCATION CENTRE

KARLSBAD
WIEN

Ungar

I. KOHLMARKT 20

NEUWELT
WIEN I.
ROTENTURMSTR. 18.

HOFSCHNEIDER

S. GUT

WIEN, VI.
GUMPENDORFERSTR. 10

Heinrich Grünbaum
Wien

Smetana
Dresden

Rhein Theater-Costüm-Fabrik
Cahn & David
DÜSSELDORF

GEBR. WOLFF & KELLER
Jerusalemer- Strasse 22
BERLIN, C.

HERMANN
Gerson
BERLIN

Braun
BERLIN - WIEN - KARLSBAD
k. u. k. Hof-Lieferanten

L. WEIN
WIEN I.
Kärntnerstr. 27

HERRMANN HOFFMANN.
Hoflieferant
BERLIN SW
von Alvensleben
Herr. Gust
No. 1910

Heinrich
Grünbaum
Wien I
Graben 26
Karlsbad
AlteWiese

Jacob
Rothberger
I. Stefansplatz 9
Wien

HELLO
GRABEN 14

N*JSRAEL
BERLIN C2

PARIS-BERLIN
KNIZE
WIEN-KARLSBAD

HERR............................
....

Dedicated to the memory of Paul Meyer and Leonore Freiman, expelled from the German and Austrian fashion industry due to the Nazi persecution of Jews.

The M. Meyer & Company in Cologne, producers and distributors of fine lace, was targeted on *Kristallnacht*. The business was later Aryanized. Leonore Ehrlich Freiman was expelled from the Michelbeuern Fashion School one week after Hitler marched into Vienna because she was Jewish.

FACING PAGE: Sketch by Leonore Freiman while a student at Michelbeuernschule, Vienna. Late 1930s.

This publication grew out of the groundbreaking exhibition *Broken Threads: The Destruction of the Jewish Fashion Industry in Germany and Austria* produced by the Vancouver Holocaust Education Centre in partnership with the Original Costume Museum Society of Vancouver in 1999. This exhibition featured the unique world-class collection assembled by Claus Jahnke of period clothing made or designed by Jewish designers. Fashion historians and collectors Claus Jahnke and Ivan Sayers served as co-curator and curiatorial assistant for this exhibition with Dr. Roberta Kremer, who created the Holocaust context and content for the exhibition.

This publication was produced through the Morris & Yosef Wosk Family Publishing Fund of the VHEC. Additional sponsorship was provided by Dick Haft, Max Fugman, Sandy Hayden and Karen Simkin. Appreciation to Karla Marks and Penny Sprackman who worked on the realization of this publication.

First published in 2007 by
Berg
Editorial offices:
1st Floor, Angel Court, 81 St Clements Street, Oxford OX4 1LJ, UK
175 Fifth Avenue, New York, NY 10010, USA

Editor: Roberta S. Kremer
Design and typesetting: Susan Mavor, Isabelle Swiderski, Metaform Communication Design
Photography credits: Marty Tessler, Graham Sharpe
Production Coordinator: Jan Selman
Copy editing and research: Jan Selman
Production support: Ronnie Tessler, Graham Sharpe, and Jennifer Fillingham
Translations: John Gort, Steven Taubeneck, and Alistair Mackay

Broken Threads: The Destruction of the Jewish Fashion Industry in Germany and Austria
Copyright © Vancouver Holocaust Education Centre 2006

Berg is the imprint of Oxford International Publishers Ltd.

Library of Congress Cataloging-in-Publication Data

A catalogue record for this book is available from the Library of Congress.

British Library Cataloguing-in-Publication Data

A catalogue record for this book is available from the British Library.

ISBN-13   978 1 84520 660 4
ISBN-10   1 84520 660 6

Printed in the UK

www.bergpublishers.com

Contents

10   Introduction – The Holocaust and Cultural Loss
Dr. Roberta S. Kremer

18   From Rags to Riches – Jews as Producers and
Purveyors of Fashion
Dr. Christopher R. Friedrichs

28   Architecture of the German Department Store
Dr. Christian Schramm
Translation by John Gort

48   Contributions of Jewish Fashion Designers in Berlin
Dr. Ingrid Loschek
Translation by John Gort

76   The Destruction of a Culture and an Industry
Dr. Irene Guenther

98   Fashion Disappears from Germany
Dr. Charlotte Schallié
Translation by Dr. Steven Taubeneck

110   Ridding Vienna's Fashion and Textile Industry of Jews
During the Nazi Period
Dr. Gloria Sultano
Translation by Alistair Mackay

Preface

This collection of essays grew out of a landmark exhibition, *Broken Threads: From Aryanization to Cultural Loss – The Destruction of the Jewish Fashion Industry in Germany and Austria,* produced by the Vancouver Holocaust Education Centre in association with The Original Costume Museum Society in 1999.

The *Broken Threads* exhibition featured the period clothing of Vancouver collector Claus Jahnke, who combined a passion for history with an interest in textiles to build an important body of historic fashionable and recreational garments and accessories made in Germany and Austria. A significant aspect of the Jahnke collection is material relating directly to the Jewish designers, retailers and manufacturers who played an important role in the German-Austrian fashion scene prior to World War II.

This was the first exhibition to feature clothing produced by Jewish high fashion designers and manufacturers in Germany and Austria prior to the Holocaust. By showing this exceptional collection in a Holocaust museum, framed by images of Nazi propaganda, boycotts, humiliation, and Aryanization, the moral issues of the Holocaust, especially the concept of cultural loss and the unresolved issues of restitution, could be publicly addressed.

In our quest to find new ways of describing the effects of the
Holocaust on society and to create new audiences for Holocaust
education, the exquisite clothing produced by Jewish firms and
designers placed alongside the cultural loss associated with
Aryanization and Nazi policies was a unique pairing. The
exhibition provided audiences with a startling contrast – colorful
creativity against the backdrop of discrimination and destruction.
The potential for this pairing was recognized by former
Vancouver Holocaust Education Centre Executive Director,
Ronnie Tessler, who encouraged a collaboration between the
Centre and collector Claus Jahnke, assisted by fashion historian
Ivan Sayers, both associated with The Original Costume Museum
Society. Tessler saw that with a comprehensive historical context,
the elegant clothing could describe both the prominence and
the destruction of Jewish involvement in the clothing industry.

Research for the exhibition brought co-curators Dr. Roberta
Kremer and Claus Jahnke to ask: Why has Jewish involvement
in the *"schmata"* and clothing trades been so prominent over
time? Why did the Nazis target the clothing industry, and
what effect did the destruction of the Jewish fashion trades,

ABOVE AND LEFT: *Broken Threads* exhibition at the Vancouver Holocaust Education Centre, January 1999.

merchandising and manufacturing have on German and Austrian fashion? How can we determine which of the leading fashion firms in Berlin and Vienna were Jewish-owned? What happened to Jewish designers and manufacturers during this period?

Determined to promote interest in this topic, stimulate research and therefore pay tribute to the outstanding contribution of Jewish talent to the German and Austrian pre-war fashion industry, essays were secured from international scholars with expertise in this field. By nature of the topic, the authors are drawn from diverse disciplines: Holocaust and Jewish Studies, Fashion History, Social History, Architecture, and German Studies.

Through these essays attention will be given to both the achievements and contributions of Jewish designers in the high fashion industry and the destruction of their involvement, in order to more fully understand the devastating cultural effects of National Socialism and the resulting Holocaust.

Roberta S. Kremer
Editor

Biblical Times
Jewish dyers and weavers enjoy high status and hold special places within the temple.

Diaspora
Tailoring skills migrate with families following the destruction of the Second Temple in Jerusalem in 70 A.D. Jews find a niche in the repair and trade of used clothing.

1295
Weavers of Berlin are forbidden to buy yarn from Jews.

1348
Jews are blamed for the Plague in Berlin and expelled from the city. It is the first of repeated expulsions and re-admissions.

15th Century
Prussia forbids Jews to enter many professions, own land or join trade guilds. They can earn a meager living trading in used clothes and tailoring.

1644
In Vienna, Christian tailors complain Jewish tailors are making ready-to-wear garments and employing Christian sewers.

1

2

3

17th Century
German tailors protest Jewish peddlers selling new clothes at Leipzig fairs and other markets.

1871
Jews achieve full emancipation with the unification of Germany, gaining access to social, cultural and economic life.

1881–83, 1903–05
Pogroms force mass emigration of Jews from Eastern Europe to Western Europe, especially Berlin and Vienna.

19th Century
German Jews establish department stores and move into large-scale manufacturing of clothing.

1920s
Berlin Jews are very prominent in fashion and culture.

1929
Jews own half of the German clothing manufacturing firms, especially in *konfektion,* the ready-to-wear branch of the industry.

1933
Germany is home to over 100,000 Jewish-owned enterprises – over half of them retail clothing stores. Many achieve success as *haute couture* designers.

4

5

IMAGES

1 Junkman, for the letter J, Italian children's book, c. 1700s.
2. Natan Wolf Lewkowicz in his tailor shop, Bedzin, Poland.
   SOURCE: USHMM Archives, courtesy of Irving and Lita Berk
3 Upper sales floors of the Tietz department store, Berlin. c. 1910.
   SOURCE:
4 Fashionplate: Afternoon suits, *Wiener Chic* (Vienna Style), magazine, 1896.
   SOURCE: C. Jahnke Collection
5 Knize storefront, Vienna.

1933

First Nazi law to make Aryan descent a condition for public employment. Soon, the same condition applies to self-employed doctors and lawyers. Jewish doctors, downgraded to "medical practitioners," can only treat other Jews. Schools and universities are Aryanized. Jewish children are denied access to public education.

Laws exclude Jews from the arts, literature, music and journalism at an editorial level. Nazi party members and government employees are prohibited from buying in Jewish-owned stores.

April 1, 1933

The first state-directed boycott against Jewish business is held. Jewish stores continue to be targeted after the Nazi-organized "official" one-day boycott. SA and Hitler Youth members are stationed outside stores, armed with anti-Semitic posters. Julius Streicher, editor of *Der Stürmer,* leads the campaign against Nuremberg's Schocken store.

1934

A questionnaire sent out to all clothing establishments asks to what extent they are Aryan. Measures are put in place to facilitate the transfer of the Jewish clothing businesses to new Aryan owners.

1935

Newspapers are forbidden to publish advertisements for Jewish enterprises. Certain park benches in Berlin's Tiergarten are painted yellow, for Jewish use only. Nuremburg Laws reclassify Jews as second-class citizens. Sexual relationships between Jew and non-Jew are forbidden. Aryan women under age 45 are forbidden to work as domestics in Jewish households.

Within fashion circles, ADEFA is not taken seriously. Their fashion shows are disappointing and poorly attended.

1936

ADEFA forms special committees: exhibits, membership, fashion shows, advertising, press, export, finance and technical. They offer Aryans incentives to join, access to the plundering of Jewish stores and the credit lines to "purchase" and operate them.

3

1

2

1938

ADEBE, a branch organization of ADEFA, is set up to control the Aryanization of the weaving and leather trades.

April 27, 1938

Göring orders the registration of all Jewish businesses, bank balances, accounts and real estate holdings. The sale of a Jewish-owned business is forbidden without permission of the Nazis. 60% to 70% of Jewish businesses in Germany have been liquidated. Of 50,000 retail stores that existed in 1933, only 9,000 remain.

1939

Clothing manufacturing is *"Judenrein"* (free of Jews) as the result of massive pressures – boycotts, sanctions, persecution – and emigration of countless Jews.

1942

Nuremberg Jewish *Gemeinde* (Community) is sent the following order: "Jews are to surrender to the authorities all fur items still in Jewish possession, including the smallest fur articles as well as collars and trimmings, even if the article of clothing is made unwearable by removal of the fur... We expect members to check their closets and wardrobes carefully to make sure not even the smallest fur articles remain. Non-compliance will be punished by the severest measures by the state police."

1945

Germany has lost the war. The country was in ruins. Money was virtually valueless and new clothing is out of the question. Even after the currency reform of 1948, most Germans are still re-fashioning old clothes, with the help of courses and "how-to" manuals.

5

4

IMAGES

1 Vienna, 1938: following the annexation of Austria. A young boy is forced to paint "Jew" on the wall of his father's store.
SOURCE: Archiv für Kunst und Geschichte (AKG), Vienna, 1938.

2 SA guard stands in front of the Jewish-owned Tietz department store in Berlin during the April 1, 1933 boycott with a sign that reads: "Germans! Defend yourselves! Do not buy from Jews!"
SOURCE: USHMM Archives

3 SA pickets wearing boycott signs block the entrance to a Jewish-owned shop in Berlin during the April 1, 1933 boycott. The signs read: "Germans defend yourselves against the Jewish atrocity propaganda: buy only at German shops!" and "Germans! Defend yourselves! Do not buy from Jews!"
SOURCE: USHMM Archives

4 Destroyed Jewish shops in Berlin, November 11, 1938.
SOURCE: Wiener Library, London

5 Warehouse of clothes confiscated from Jews who perished in Auschwitz-Birkenau, 1945.
SOURCE: USHMM Archives

"Central Europe in the years before Hitler owed much to the Jewish genius – more than perhaps any other part of the world. The Jews were the 'intellectual cement,' the cosmopolitan and integrative element which added a quintessentially European color, tone and vitality to great cities like Berlin, Vienna, Prague and Budapest."

Milan Kundera

The Holocaust and Cultural Loss

Roberta S. Kremer

Writing on the Holocaust has focused primarily on the personal suffering of those targeted by the Nazis and the brutality done to the victims. What has not been as fully explored within Holocaust discourse is the resulting cultural loss, which by its very nature is vast, more abstract and much harder to measure.

Cultural loss ensues when traditions, values, language, and other features that distinguish one group of people from other groups, or form a minority within a larger cultural group, are destroyed. Destruction of culture can occur from a variety of forces – through forced migration, assimilation, dislocation and colonialism – but always accompanies genocide. Cultural loss resulting from the Holocaust includes the music, literature, and art, as well as the accomplishments in science and medicine never to be realized. It includes the inventions, designs, and architecture that will never be realized on European soil, with a uniquely European flavor and orientation.

Between 1933 and 1945 the Nazis, by murdering six million Jews, also systematically destroyed the flourishing Jewish urban communities in most major cities of Europe as well as hundreds of small Jewish *shtetls*. The loss of European Jewish intellectual history as reflected in religious, social and cultural traditions

Cultural Loss
When a specific people are destroyed, the unique music that composers would have written, the books, the inventions, designs, painting, poetry, medical cures and advances that would have been, are also destroyed. This loss is a loss for all time. Humanity is permanently diminished.

Aryanization
The process of removing all non-Aryan persons from office, business and cultural life. (In Nazi doctrine, Aryan referred to a non-Jewish Caucasian, especially of Nordic stock.)

came to a complete and permanent end, depriving future generations of a rich and complex cultural inheritance.

When the contributions of a group are lost through genocide, apartheid or discrimination, there is an unrecoverable loss to the larger society. Empty of their Jewish citizens, Germany and Austria permanently destroyed an essential part of their own cultural identity. Not only were the Jewish communities as unique segments destroyed but also the very nature and flavor of the European cities they inhabited was inexorably altered.

What the perpetrators lost as a result of the Holocaust is a subject not often addressed by the countries that carried out the Final Solution. As German Foreign Minister Joschka Fischer stated in *Die Zeit* in 2003: "The real issue – which we have not even begun to debate as yet is this: What have we done to ourselves? And what have we lost as a result? The destruction of European Jewry amounts also to the destruction of our own German culture."

The achievements of German Jews had long brought international prestige and fame to Germany. German Jews were especially prominent in music, literature, architecture, science and medicine. Germany had many Nobel Prize winners, world-famous artists,

pioneering researchers, and independent thinkers, all contributing to an international reputation that to a significant extent was based on the achievements of German-Jews.

Nearly half a million Jews lived in Germany and Austria when Hitler came to power. Approximately 300,000 left to find refuge elsewhere; over 210,000 perished. Austrian Jews such as Sigmund Freud, Elias Canetti, Stefan Zweig and Arnold Schönberg were forced to end their careers elsewhere. Writers and poets such as Else Lasker-Schüler and Lion Feuchtwanger defined a generation, greatly influencing the world of German literature. Musicians Otto Klemperer and Bruno Walter, as well as scientists Albert Einstein, Max Born and Lise Meitner, recognized internationally for their achievements, were all forced out of Germany. With the expulsion and murder of their great Jewish artists and thinkers, Germany and Austria permanently destroyed a part of their "own" cultural fabric, a part of their own soul.

The essays in this publication explore and describe through the lens of fashion the contribution of Jews and address questions of cultural loss to Germany and Austria. The essays examine the contributions of Jewish designers, clothing manufacturers

and merchandisers to fashion trends in Germany and Austria and the effect of their expulsion on the fashion industry.

Although clothing and fashion may appear as an unusual lens through which to look at the destruction of European Jewry, it is important to note that the Nazis themselves made it a central issue. Identified as being in Jewish hands, the fashion industry was strongly associated with Jewish commerce and talent, and therefore specifically targeted by the Nazis for destruction. Almost 80 percent of department and chain store businesses in pre-war Germany were Jewish-owned, as were 40 percent of wholesale textile firms, and 60 percent of wholesale and retail clothing businesses. All the major Berlin department stores – Wertheim, Herman Tietz, Nathan Israel, KaDeWe – were the property of Jews. By 1895, 56 percent of German Jews were involved in commerce while only 10 percent of non-Jewish Germans were in this field.

An examination of fashion in even one period of European history is a complex interdisciplinary study in social history. Class, gender, age and economic aspirations, as well as morality and patriotism are all reflected in clothing. Fashion is a tangible manifestation as well as a fluid and dynamic process

since it responds quickly to social, economic and political
conditions, both reflecting and influencing changes in style
and design.

The first essay chronicles the rise in prominence of Jewish
merchants, clothing designers and manufacturers in Germany
and Austria, a prominence that existed for over a hundred years.
Later essays describe in detail how in a short period of time
Nazism changed that forever. Forced from their homes and
businesses, excluded from occupations and cultural life, Jews
disappeared from Europe. Along with their disappearance went
the fashion prominence of Berlin and Vienna. Other essays in
this collection describe the targeting of this industry and its
systematic unraveling, addressing both the contributions and
the total annihilation of the majority of Jews involved in nearly
all aspects of the clothing trades as well as the consequences
for German and Austrian fashion prominence.

Essays also discuss the role of dislocation, immigration and
the Diaspora of Jewish talent and the families involved in the
fashion enterprises. Most perished, only a few escaped. Of
those who survived most were never able to re-establish their
fashion careers or their businesses. Some immigrated to new

countries where significant differences in fashion proved to be insurmountable barriers to resuming careers. Others created a "fashion Diaspora"– a scattering – as those designers and manufacturers who could escape, left Germany and Austria and made important contributions to the clothing trades in places as far afield as Tel Aviv, Toronto, Hollywood and London. Prevented from working in Nazi Germany, Erich Mendelsohn, architect of the great German department stores, left for England just prior to the outbreak of war, leaving everything he owned behind. He continued to design buildings in England and later in the United States and in Israel. Like many other talented Jewish artists, Mendelsohn chose not to return to Germany after the war.

The Nazi years put an end to the century-old blossoming of Jewish culture and life in Europe. Germany eliminated an essential contributing group to its own national identity. The expulsion and murder of European Jewry left a human and cultural void that cannot be filled.

1263

Mode Journal „Wiener Chic."

Herausgeber

B. Finkelstein & Bruder

XVIII. Witthauergasse 26 im eigenen Hause.

...er B. Finkelstein & Bruder.

Kunstdruckerei v. R...

From Rags to Riches –
Jews as Producers and Purveyors of Fashion

Christopher R. Friedrichs

At the end of the eighteenth century, the typical image of a Jew in Germany or Austria might have been that of a ragpicker or peddler travelling from place to place selling old fabrics and used clothing.

By the early twentieth century, the typical image of a German or Austrian Jew might well have been that of the owner of a fashionable dress shop or department store in Berlin or Vienna waiting respectfully on German ladies of high social rank as they selected their gowns and outfits for the coming season. All too soon, of course, that picture would change once again. Just a generation later, the same stores and shops would have been closed down or placed under new management and the owners and their families would find themselves living in exile or, in some cases, facing deportation to be murdered in Hitler's extermination camps. This tragic end of the story must never be overlooked, but before one can understand how the flourishing German Jewish involvement in the world of high fashion came to such a bitter end one must know something about why Jews came to enter that world in the first place.

The society of Germany and Austria changed enormously between the late eighteenth and early twentieth centuries –

Pogrom
An organized massacre, especially of Jews.

Itinerant Jewish peddlers traveled from town to town, selling used clothing from middle and upper class homes to farmers and townspeople, and contributing to the migration of fashion styles. As they traveled, Jewish peddlers disseminated news, humour and stories.

At the turn of the century, anti-Semitic pogroms in eastern Europe forced even greater numbers of Jews into urban centres like Berlin and Vienna. They brought their skills in the needle trades with them. Historically excluded by law from many professions and guilds, Jews gravitated to the 'rag' or *schmata* trade. Their skill as tailors, furriers, seamstresses, hat makers and designers, combined with 19th century legal reforms, led to new opportunities.

and so, even more dramatically, did the position of Jews in that society. Jews had lived in many of the territories and principalities of central Europe since the Middle Ages, but until the eighteenth century their position was weak and insecure. A long tradition of Christian anti-Semitism along with constant fears of the Jews' economic potential accounted for the fact that Jews were permitted to live in the German and Austrian lands only under severe restrictions. Jews could dwell only in certain communities and could practice only certain trades. They had one advantage: by moving into the economic niche originally created in the Middle Ages when Christians were still forbidden to lend money at interest, a handful of Jews became wealthy as moneylenders, bankers and financiers. But most Jews were poor. In every town where they lived they had to confront the fact that the powerful trade associations known as guilds were determined to maintain their economic monopolies. Each trade or craft could only be practiced by members of the relevant guild – and Jews were never admitted to these organizations. True, Jews could make and sell wares to be used by members of their own community, but they were strictly forbidden to make goods to be sold on the open market. No Jew could weave cloth, make shoes or sew clothing to be worn by Christians.

BALL TOILETTE.

There was one loophole, however: Jews were generally allowed to sell recycled goods. Accordingly, many Jews tried to earn a living by peddling second-hand products. Since textiles and clothing were the most important manufactured goods in pre-industrial times, it is hardly surprising that many Jews specialized in selling used items of apparel. Thus, although they were forbidden to deal in new clothing, Jews did acquire considerable experience in the clothing market.

The long-established position of Jews in German society began to change in the eighteenth century. A major impetus was provided by the liberating doctrines of the Enlightenment, whose leaders believed that social progress required an atmosphere of religious and economic freedom. Many of these principles were implemented in the German states during the tumultuous years of the French Revolution and the Napoleonic wars between 1789 and 1815. It was in these years that in some parts of Germany the Jews began to experience the process of legal emancipation. Many of the economic restrictions under which Jews had suffered were lifted, and Jews began to practice trades from which they had been barred for hundreds of years. Even so, the economic and social emancipation of the Jews in

Germany and Austria was a piecemeal process. After the defeat of Napoleon some reforms were canceled, only to be restored a few decades later. And each of the different German states introduced changes at its own pace. It was not until Germany was finally unified in 1871 that Jews all over the German Empire enjoyed full and equal legal and economic rights. In Austria full emancipation had occurred just a few years earlier, in 1867.

While historians agree that the Jews of Germany and Austria were fully emancipated by 1871, they are less certain about the degree to which Jews were fully assimilated. Most German Jews were eager to adopt a lifestyle similar to that of their Christian neighbors and confident that they could do so without surrendering their Jewish religion and cultural heritage. In language, dress and education, most German Jews by the late nineteenth century were entirely Germanized. Yet subtle barriers still prevented their full integration into German society. Anti-Semitism had never fully disappeared, and in fact it was on the rise again by the late nineteenth century. Social mixing between Christians and Jews was still limited. And some professions were, for all practical purposes, still inaccessible to Jews. At the end of the nineteenth century, for example, Jews in Germany still found it hard to become judges or university professors – and almost

In 1860, Vienna was home to 6,200 Jews. By 1900, more than 147,000 Jews lived in Austria's sophisticated cultural centre. Ten years later, another 70,000 Eastern Jews had settled in German cities—one quarter in the capital city of Berlin. Two-thirds worked in some aspect of the garment industry—mostly in family-owned businesses.

Many women at home worked in the *Konfektion* (ready-to-wear clothing) industry. In 1910, when a Berlin teacher asked, "What do your mothers do after you go to bed at night?", most students replied "My mother sews dresses," "My grandmother sews linings in jackets," or "My aunt sews blouses."

RIGHT: Natan Wolf Lewkowicz in his tailor shop.
SOURCE: USHMM Archives, courtesy of Irving and Lita Berk

FACING PAGE: Label from men's court breeches by Hermann Hoffmann. Hermann Hoffmann was in business from 1897 to 1938, when the store was Aryanized.
SOURCE: C. Jahnke Collection

BELOW: Grunfeld fabric store.
SOURCE: Leo Baeck Institute

impossible to become diplomats or military officers.

In economic life, however, the barriers were completely gone. Throughout the nineteenth century Jewish entrepreneurs embraced the commercial opportunities presented by the elimination of anti-Jewish restrictions and the growing popularity of free-market doctrines. Not surprisingly, one of the key areas of Jewish activity was in the garment trades, the economic sector in which Jews had long enjoyed an established if peripheral role. By the 1830s, some Jewish firms in Berlin were selling a variety of elegant new cloth fabrics. Within a few years Jewish clothiers had expanded their activities to include the sale of finished coats and other garments made by tailors working under their supervision. By the end of the nineteenth century, Jewish clothiers were a fixture in countless German and Austrian cities.

Jews also participated in the development of one of the most creative new institutions of the nineteenth century: the department store. Until the early nineteenth century, most goods were still manufactured by hand and sold in the workshops where they had been produced. With the growing complexity of the manufacturing process, however, the point of sale increasingly became detached from the place of manufacture. Soon

Early in the 1930s Germany's economic recovery started. Suddenly

> "Early in the 1930s Germany's economic recovery started. Suddenly people had money after the dreary Depression years and they wanted to have a good time and to spend it on luxury items."
>
> Paul Meyer, M. Meyer & Company

there were general stores which sold a variety of dry goods. Eventually some of them evolved further into true department stores. In Germany many of them were founded by Jews.

The development of the Israel family's involvement in the clothing business in Berlin can be taken as an example of this pattern. In 1741 the king of Prussia granted Israel Jacob the right to live in Berlin. After a quarter of a century of selling used garments and laces from an open stall, Israel Jacob finally accumulated enough wealth to buy a house in Berlin and operate his business on a more permanent basis. In 1815 his grandson Nathan Israel took advantage of liberalized economic laws to open a firm which eventually began to sell both new and used clothing as well as trading in fabrics. By now, Israel had been adopted as the family name. Nathan's son and grandson steadily expanded the business. By the early twentieth century, their firm had developed into one of Berlin's greatest department stores, which specialized in direct and mail-order sales of linens and clothing and tailoring of fine garments but also offered furniture and housewares. By the 1930s the N. Israel department store was one of the largest and most versatile commercial enterprises in Berlin.

Ladies Day at the Berlin Races, 1930. The women are wearing clothing by Becker, a couture house in the centre of Berlin. SOURCE: *Berlin Between the Wars*, Thomas Friedrich, photo by Ullstein.

The great blossoming of Berlin culture ranged from music, avant garde art, fashion and theatre to cinema, intellectual salons and cabarets. People had a reason to dress well. This was the era of Kurt Weill's *The Threepenny Opera,* graphic satirist George Grosz, Dada artist Kurt Schwittters, composer Richard Strauss, Bauhaus architect Walter Gropius, Fritz Lang's film *Metropolis,* and Marlene Dietrich's *The Blue Angel.* In 1928, Berlin offered readers 2,633 newspapers and periodicals, many with arts coverage. Theatre critic Altred Kerr of the *Berliner Tageblatt* was a household name. Berlin was the undisputed leader in both photo journalism and art photography. There were scores of public and private schools where the next generation of artists, including fashion designers, could train.

ABOVE: Evening soirée, Berlin, 1934.
SOURCE: Ewald Hoinkis, photographer

Jews had reached the pinnacle of the German garment and fashion industry by the early twentieth century, but their position in this as in so many other aspects of German and Austrian life was far from secure. Indeed, the very prominence of Jewish leaders in the garment and fashion sectors was exploited, like other forms of Jewish achievement, by the proponents of anti-Semitic ideas throughout Germany

OPPOSITE PAGE: *Der Stürmer,* January 18, 1938.

BELOW: Anti-Semitic election poster for the German political party, *The Völkischer Block,* 1928.
SOURCE: Wiener Library, London

LOWER LEFT: After Kristallnacht, Berlin, November 9-10, 1938.
SOURCE: AKG

and Austria in the late nineteenth and early twentieth centuries. Any manifestation of Jewish economic success could become a target of the anti-Semites. In addition, as the racist underpinnings of anti-Semitism became increasingly blatant, there emerged a scarcely disguised antipathy to the idea that Jewish clothiers and tailors should be responsible for creating the clothes that draped the bodies of German women. When the Nazis came to power in 1933, such attitudes suddenly became the basis for state policy. Within just a few years, the participation of Jews in the economic life of Germany and Austria had been destroyed. The N. Israel department store, for example, shared the fate of countless other Jewish enterprises: during the Kristallnacht pogrom of November 1938, Nazi thugs attacked the store and destroyed huge amounts of merchandise. By February 1939, in accordance with Nazi decrees, ownership of the store had been transferred to a non-Jewish firm. The creative contribution that Jews had made to the garment and fashion industry of Germany and Austria was crushed out of existence. And if the Nazis had had their way, this aspect of Jewish achievement would by now have been forgotten – but in this, at least, the Nazis failed.

Architecture of the German Department Store

Christian Schramm
Translated from the German by John Gort

ORIGINS OF THE DEPARTMENT STORE

An investigation into the origins of department store architecture and the construction-historical classification of these buildings can only be carried out within the proper social, economic and technical contexts. To examine the architectural prototype of the German department store, we must turn to the oriental bazaar rather than to the arcade. The invention of this type of building as the *grande magazins* in France stood for a totally new style of retail business and is of great importance in understanding the development of similar architecture that occurred somewhat later in a decentralized Germany.

In 1869 the Parisian merchant Boucicaut opened the department store *An Bon Marche*, generally acknowledged in the literature as the first true department store. The enormous economic success of this new concept, with its low prices, small profit margins paired with high turnover, and with better utilization of the building site through the use of upper floors, made increasingly larger buildings necessary. By 1888 *An Bon Marche* had expanded to a floor space of 10,000 square meters. Its architecture revelled in historicism; its debt to the previously

built Paris Opera House is apparent in both the interior design and in the outside appearance of the building.

The design of the department store took its bearings from the buildings of the World's Fair. The London Crystal Palace (1851), with its "Iron-Glass" architecture, exerted a powerful influence on all important construction projects, reaching its highest point with the construction of the Paris department store *Printemps* in 1889. This type of building was an example for all of Europe that retained its general validity until 1918; it was characterized by halls and several floors, entrances through generous well-lit stairways and galleries, large inner courts, framed construction with palace-like stone facades and large windows.

ORIGIN AND DEVELOPMENT OF THE DEPARTMENT STORE IN
GERMANY BEFORE THE FIRST WORLD WAR

At a time when the new "Shopping Places" of Paris were already fully developed, no evolution of that sort had as yet occurred in Germany. As in the delay of industrialization in Germany, the growth of German department stores was slower than in France. The establishment of firms occurred in provincial cities with the formation of a network of branches: in 1876, Wertheim in Stralsund; in 1881, Karstadt in Wismar; and in 1882, Tietz in Gera.

Herrmann Gerson's second store, built in 1849, was the first building in Berlin designed specifically as a department store. The central skylight, flooding the store with daylight, was soon a standard feature in department store design. Window dressing became an art form.

LEFT: Gerson department store, 19th Century.
SOURCE: *Berliner Konfektion und Mode*

RIGHT: Show and sales room of Gerson.
SOURCE: *Berliner Konfektion und Mode*

BELOW: Gerson advertisement.
SOURCE: C. Jahnke Collection

PREVIOUS SPREAD: The fabric department at Wertheim, Berlin.
SOURCE: BPK

The most important items for sale in these businesses were dry goods, clothing and haberdashery. As late as 1877 the manual of the Berlin Society of Architects stated:

> *For a long time only the fashion firm House Gerson on the Werder Markt and the building of the haberdashery firm House Israel on Spandau Street have remained as the only substantive examples of structures specifically designed for the sole purpose of serving the retail trade.*

Gerson and Valentin Manheimer, both Jewish, were driven by founding ambitions. Between 1840 and 1870 they created the foundation for a rapidly expanding ready-to-wear ladies' dress business. By 1894 the House Gerson was the largest enterprise in that trade. Nathan Israel's firm was among the most important fashion houses of the ready-to wear manufacturers of ladies' clothing in Berlin. In the thirties this firm employed two thousand workers. The enterprise was known as the counterpart of Harrods in London.

In 1884 the four brothers Wertheim risked a move to Berlin. Just as in Paris, the fashion houses developed out of dry goods and haberdashery stores. Only after many firms had settled in the emerging world-class city of Berlin, which at that time offered all the necessary technical and social conditions, were circumstances favourable for the development of department stores. The French *grands magazins* undoubtedly served as prototypes. The decisive step for the future of German department store architecture was the construction of the Wertheim department store on Leipzig Street. The architect Alfred Messel planned this building in three phases: 1897, 1900 and 1906. Following further expansion in 1912 and 1927, it became Europe's largest department store. The design of this "first of the German department stores" provided the generally accepted formula for the typical department store facade. Sculptured protruding masonry pillars used as main supports helped overcome the horizontal stratification of the floors. Expanses of walls were not to be seen; instead there were expanses of glass with filigree-like iron constructions. The structure consisted of an airy system of pillars of the smallest dimension possible, placed as far apart as possible, with the ceilings clamped between the pillars like fixed horizontal panels. A wide gallery-like glass-roofed court brought the whole concept into focus and formed its center, combining the whole five floors into one large exhibition hall with a skylight.

The modern department store created a new, luxurious style of shopping. The physical design altered the shape and size of stores, offering services previously only available to the wealthy. The chain store was another new concept, beginning in 1908 with H. Tietz. Berlin was home to flagship stores of many department store chains.

BELOW: Tietz department store, 1910. Cremer and Wolffenstein, Architect.

FOLLOWING PAGES: Tietz department store, 1910.
SOURCE: BPK

Up to the outbreak of World War I many department stores, built according to the pattern of the Wertheim design, emerged in many large and medium-sized German cities. These stores helped to decide the character of the city and determined in many places the definitive trends of the architectural development in the core of the inner city. The department store Tietz on the Alexanderplatz (1905) serves as an example of this influence:

> *The migration to the west that occurred in Berlin caused the Alexanderplatz to fall into desolation. The streets that bordered on the Alexanderplatz towards the west became a region of wholesalers; however the streets leading towards the east, south and north degenerated into the worst slums in all of Berlin ... all Berliners shook their heads in disbelief and considered father's determination to build a department store in this godforsaken spot on the Alexanderplatz as the ultimate stupidity. Father refused to discuss this matter; sometimes he laughed and replied abruptly: 'Location – that, I will create!'*

During World War I the building industry stagnated. No new
department stores were planned. Since the state-controlled
economy of the war years did not permit free competition –
the most important prerequisite for successful department
stores – but rather encouraged the rise of a pure sellers'
market, that period must be viewed as a time of stagnation of
further development of department store design.

New approaches to merchandising created a retail revolution. Prices and sizes were fixed. A wide range of merchandise was offered. Customers were encouraged to browse. Credit was offered and goods could be returned.

LEFT: The carpet department of the Tietz department store. Berlin, 1909.
SOURCE: BPK

RIGHT: Tietz "ascending staircase", c. 1925.
SOURCE: BPK

FURTHER DEVELOPMENT OF THE DEPARTMENT STORE AFTER 1920

The period between 1920 and 1940 is divided into three parts. First was a period of international economic expansion (with the exception of Germany) from the end of World War I up to 1929. During this time the prosperity experienced all over the world affected almost all areas of the standard of living. The second phase was the period of economic crisis between 1930 and 1933. Between 1929 and 1933, turnover in the retail trade declined by 40 percent both in the United States and in Germany. The third phase included the development that took place during the era of National Socialism after 1933.

Only after 1924 did Germany take part in the universal economic boom. The period just after 1924 was a time of mergers, like those that occurred in the German industrial firms of IG Farben and Vereinigte Stahlwerke. Between 1926 and 1929, the five largest department stores, Karstadt, Kaufhof, Tietz, Wertheim and Schocken, all grew into large-scale enterprises employing 10,000 - 20,000 people. Despite the acquisition of 79 existing firms between 1924 and 1929, mergers and acquisitions resulted in only eleven new buildings being erected by large enterprises. Apart from the decision to merge, large firms tried to grow by expanding into other types of businesses. In anticipation of F.W. Woolworth opening branches in Germany, Tietz opened the first Ehape branch store (later called Kaufhalle).

Tied to the expansion into related areas of trade was the introduction of organizational techniques. Thus Salman Schocken, the great organizer and creator of an important economic enterprise (with a turnover of 100 million marks during 1931) considered the fact that his business operated along scientific guidelines as the principal secret of his success. The organization of his enterprise was based on the principle of strict centralization.

From the start Salman Schocken placed special emphasis on the architecture of his department stores. It was his goal that the facade, layout and interior design conformed to the special requirements of the building in every detail, and that it meet the standards that modern architecture had developed for special purpose buildings. Even during the years before World War I, he had published essays on the development of department stores in Germany and on the economics of building department stores as well as on the architecture of department stores.

ABOVE: Kaufhaus, Petersdorff by Mendelsohn, November, 1929.
SOURCE: Martin Munkacsy, ullstein bild / The Granger Collection, New York

LEFT: Kaufhaus Schocken, Stuttgart by Mendelsohn,1928.
SOURCE: ullstein bild / The Granger Collection, New York

In Erich Mendelsohn, the designer of the great Schocken-owned department stores of the twenties, Schocken found an architect who knew how take into consideration, in a genius-like manner, the artistic point of view as well as the practical necessities. It goes without saying that Mendelsohn worked in collaboration with an owner who, in his intensity and in the dimension of his creative initiative, differed greatly from the traditional influence exerted by a building's owner.

In his lecture "The Problem of the New Architectural Art," delivered in the Workshop for Art in Berlin in 1919, Mendelsohn introduced a new era of creativity:

> *Every achievement, from the autonomous attainments of medieval architectural style and even in the creative period of the baroque until the contemporary artistic achievements of architectural form of our day, is based on the patterns of designs of the ancient principles of construction. Just as no connection exists between the principle of load and support of the ancient period and the Gothic standard of pillar and arch, either in building technology or in artistic creativity, it must be clearly recognized that the first concrete and steel*

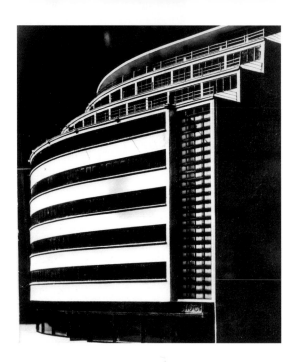

*span is no less significant than the feeling of deliver-
ance that was induced in the Middle Ages by the
triumph of the first arch over the building technology
of the ancients.*

Mendelsohn's first building created in this style, the
Einsteinturm, showed an overestimation of the contemporary
potential of concrete and steel construction. The Einsteinturm
was intended as the first realization of the "plastic" possibilities
of concrete construction; however, the basement was
brickwork covered with plaster, giving the finished building
the appearance of having been built out of concrete. Through
building the Einsteinturm, the translation of the sketch of an
idea into reality, Mendelsohn discovered that not all ideas
could be translated into practice. Mendelsohn's most brilliant
buildings were the four department stores he created between
1926 and 1929: Schocken in Nuremburg, Stuttgart, and
Chemnitz; and Petersdorff in Breslau.

Until that time department stores usually looked like clumsily
imitated Renaissance palaces with oversized store windows on
the ground floor. Mendelsohn seems to have been the first
architect to find an up-to-date solution to this modern

problem. He made the stores efficient as well as effective. His department stores demonstrated architectural exhibitionism in the best sense with their interesting and dynamic construction, their exquisite taste, and their careful attention to rich detail. Mendelsohn, probably with some debt to the Bauhaus movement, spawned the development of a new kind of department store.

Mendelsohn's designs generated totally new expressions of architectural language, replacing the notion of the "house" with the traditional lobby, upper floors and inclined roof as its highest point. Accordingly the facade underwent a radical transformation. Walls, openings, girders and loads lost their meanings as established principles. Steel-girder construction permitted large expanses of windows without numerous interruptions. The emphatically horizontal layered ribbon-like facade gained acceptance as the prototype of the department store. Mendelsohn elevated his horizontal "window-ribbons" to a dogma. At the same time he introduced a horizontal emphasis into the stairwells, with the aim of reinforcing the appearance of the whole structure.

The interior of the store was marked by a lessening emphasis and eventual elimination of the glass-roofed interior court. An

exception to this trend was the new department store built in Berlin in 1929 by Philipp Schäfer for the firm of Karstadt-Neukölln. This store was the largest department store built between the world wars and became the flagship of the Karstadt enterprise. It shows the influence of American high-rise architecture Schäfer had studied during his stay in the USA. The structure resembles Ralph Walker's trend-setting Barklay Versey building (New York, 1926). The Karstadt-Haus became the symbol of the entrepreneurial success of the firm Karstadt. Its forceful pillar-design once again raised the demand for creative continuity of the design of department stores built during the time of Kaiser Wilhelm.

The economic crisis of 1929 marked the end of the short-lived five-year boom. High unemployment, 6 million in Germany, and inner-political tensions, which resulted in low purchasing power, were causes for a decline of 41 percent in the retail trade business between 1929 and 1933.

The takeover by the National Socialists at the end of January 1933 ushered in the period of dictatorship and an increasing dissociation from events within the international economy. From the start the NSDAP looked for its base of support among

"What made the biggest impression on me as a six- or seven-year-old," recalls the great grandson of Grünfeld's founder, "was the magic fountain in the basement that dispensed lemonade instead of water."

Adults delighted in their ride up the tubular elevator-shaft of glass and chrome.

FAR LEFT: Grünfeld illustration from *Styl* magazine, 1922.
SOURCE: C. Jahnke Collection

LEFT: Elevator at Grünfeld department store.
SOURCE: Leo Baeck Institute, New York

tradespeople and members of the lower middle class. The Nazis therefore directed their propaganda against the major businesses and their mostly Jewish owners. As early as 1920 the program of the NSDAP, Section 16, demanded the transfer of department stores to public ownership:

> *We demand the creation and the support of a healthy middle class, immediate transfer to public ownership of the department stores and that they be offered to small tradesmen for rent at low cost, and that the keenest consideration be afforded to all small tradesmen when awarding contracts for deliveries to authorities of the State, the provinces and individual communities.*

Economic considerations played no role in the drafting of the Nazi Party program; all that mattered was to win votes during elections. Middle class tradesmen had not found a place in the parties of the young Weimar Republic. The NSDAP quite consciously and with instinctive certainty exploited this gap in parliamentary life. The "Problem of the Department Stores" was adopted as a political slogan because of the department stores' deliberate suppression of competition; this made them a powerful symbol that could be exploited for the unification of

Major Jewish-owned department stores

Berlin	Vienna
Nathan Israel	Jacob Rothberger
Herrmann Gerson	Gerngross
Wertheim	Goldmann & Salatsch
H. Tietz	Herzmansky
Grünfeld	Zwieback
Jandorf's Kaufhause Des Westons (K.D.W.)	

Finanzamt **Köln-Weidenbach**

St.-Nr. **451/643**

Die Namen und Unterschriftsproben der zur Quittungs-
erteilung berechtigten Beamten sind im Kassenraum
angeschlagen.

Die Finanzkasse ist für den Zahlungsverkehr geöffnet:

Kassenstunden 8–13 Uhr.
Samstags (mit Ausnahme von Fälligkeitstagen),
sowie am letzten Werktage jeden Monats geschlossen.

Köln, **12. Dez. 1938** 193

Fördert den unbaren Zahlungsverkehr, er
erspart längeres Warten in der Finanzkasse!

Das Finanzamt (Finanzkasse) hat folgende Konten:

Postscheckkonto Köln Nr. 94
Konto Nr. 17006 bei der Sparkasse der Stadt Köln
Konto Nr. 8000 b. d. Kreissparkasse d. Landkreise Köln,
Rheinisch-Bergischer Kreis und Bergheim in Köln
Reichsbank-Giro-Konto

Bescheid über die Judenvermögensabgabe

Auf Grund der Durchführungsverordnung über die Sühneleistung der Juden vom 21. November 1938
(Reichsgesetzbl. I S. 1638) wird die von Ihnen zu entrichtende Abgabe festgesetzt auf

42 800 RM

Die Abgabe beträgt 20 vom Hundert des von Ihnen auf Grund der Verordnung über die An-
meldung des Vermögens von Juden vom 26. April 1938 (Reichsgesetzbl. I S. 414) angemeldeten
Vermögens (unter Berücksichtigung angezeigter Veränderungen).

Die Abgabe ist zu entrichten in vier Teilbeträgen von je

10 700 RM

Der erste Teilbetrag ist bis zum 15. Dezember 1938,
die weiteren Teilbeträge sind bis zum 15. Februar,
15. Mai und
15. August 1939

unter Bezeichnung als Judenvermögensabgabe und unter Angabe der oben vermerkten St.-Nr. zu leisten.

Wird eine Zahlung nicht rechtzeitig entrichtet, so ist mit Ablauf des Fälligkeitstags ein Säumnis-
zuschlag in Höhe von zwei vom Hundert des rückständigen Betrags verwirkt. Nach Ablauf der
Zahlungsfrist werden rückständige Beträge ohne vorhergehende Mahnung eingezogen und erforder-
lichenfalls beigetrieben. Die Zwangsvollstreckungskosten fallen dem Zahlungspflichtigen zur Last.

Herrn/Frau *Mose Meyer*

in *Köln*

the splintered middle class under the banner of the NSDAP. After the Nazis' rise to power, the SA especially distinguished itself by unlawful transgressions against the large retail firms. Boycotts occurred, display windows were broken, and businesses were identified as having Jewish ownership. With the permission of the government, legal measures were invoked against the department stores as early as 1933. For example, higher taxes were levied on department stores and their branches, and there was a prohibition against opening, relocating or expanding department stores in Bavaria.

The economic situation of department stores became ever more critical. The value of the department store shares of the Tietz conglomerate fell from 55 percent in 1932 to 12 percent in 1933. Within a few months of the Nazis' coming to power, department stores were already on the verge of bankruptcy.

The organizational style of the department stores, with their approximately 72,000 employees, was closely entwined with that of the total economy. A liquidation of the stores and the related mass dismissals of staff would have led to catastrophic consequences. It was therefore decided by the highest authority that:

> *The position of the NSDAP vis-à-vis the department store question remains basically unchanged. The solution to this problem will be found in good time in the spirit of the National Socialist Program. In view of the general economic situation, the party leadership is considering active steps with the objective of eliminating department store-like enterprises inappropriate at this time.*

This change did not indicate a radical change in political direction – many restrictive measures continued to be implemented. The highest priority was the dislodging of Jewish proprietors and employees, in line with the rapidly expanding process of Aryanization, from their positions within the retail trade. Countless businesses owned by Jews were sold for "bargain prices" or transformed into firms directed by Aryans.

Label from bodice of theatrical costume 1890's.
SOURCE: C. Jahnke Collection

The Jewish proprietors had to choose between emigration and the road to the concentration camp.

Kristallnacht, when many Jewish businesses were plundered or destroyed, appeared to those who experienced it to be the acme of Nazi terror, yet worse was to follow. For the ordinary citizen Kristallnacht provided a new experience, that of observing the open reign of terror. But even this undisguised criminal behaviour by the Nazis was ultimately less outrageous than the crimes they committed later behind closed doors. As Kristallnacht marked the end of the development of the department store in Germany, I will not go into a description of these later atrocities. Kristallnacht initiated a period of stagnation of architectural development. During the Second World War the Aryanized department stores assumed more or less the function of distribution centres. The air raids caused the total destruction of many buildings. The division of the Reich after the war resulted in the loss of many department store branches and locations.

Contributions of Jewish Fashion Designers in Berlin

Ingrid Loschek
Translated from the German by John Gort

BERLIN — A METROPOLIS OF FASHION

During the 19th century no city in the world had perfected the manufacture of ready-to-wear clothing to the extent achieved in Berlin. Although Berlin was not a world-renowned centre of high fashion, it was the centre of the ready-to-wear industry and became an important model for the clothing industries of Paris, Vienna and London as well as New York. Berlin's pre-eminence in ready-to-wear came about through the interplay of several factors, some dating back as far as the 17th century.

In 1671 through an edict, Jews residing in the Province of Brandenburg were permitted to enter the new clothing trade. They could now engage in peddling new as well as used clothes. It was hoped that this measure would alleviate the shortage of clothes that had existed since the Thirty Years War. Jewish tailors forced to work outside the tailors' guilds had to produce much of this new clothing illegally. The ability to sell new clothing, combined with the illegal production of new clothing, made it possible for Jewish tailors to develop a new branch of the clothing trade, *Konfektion,* or ready-to-wear, lines of clothing made in standardized sizes.[1]

RIGHT: Cover, Nathan Israel catalogue, Winter 1932 with image of Leni Riefenstahl. SOURCE: C. Jahnke Collection

FACING PAGE: The Nathan Israel store, founded in 1815. Its destruction during Kristallnacht was the sacking of a Berlin institution.

LOWER FACING PAGE: Label from mens dress shirt, c 1930. SOURCE: C. Jahnke Collection

PREVIOUS SPREAD: Poster for "The Academy for Good Cutting" by Ernst Dryden, 1911.

In 1811, during an economic upturn, the Prussians bestowed upon Prussian Jews the temporary freedom to choose their trade. One year later Prussian Jews were granted more legal equality, resulting in a migration of a large number of Jews from Posen to Berlin. Among these immigrants were many tailors.[2] Also important was the dissemination of organizational knowledge and efficient production methods used in the tailoring of military uniforms in Prussia.[3] This expertise had developed during the 18th century due to the needs of the Prussian army for uniforms. The production of uniforms also involved numerous sub-contractors such as manufacturers of military braids and buttons. Thus the conditions, expertise in trade and the production of clothing, were in place in Berlin for the development of *Konfektion*.[4]

One of the first to enter the ready-to-wear business was Nathan Israel, nephew of Jacob Israel, a used clothing peddler. Nathan Israel founded his clothing business in 1815. By the turn of the century it had blossomed into one of Berlin's best-known establishments. Nathan Israel's sold everything from low-priced, off-the-rack goods to luxurious one-of-a-kind dresses. The firm remained under the family's ownership until the Nazis expropriated it in 1938.

In 1836 Herrmann Gerson[5] opened a small textile shop in the Royal Academy of Architecture, a building in the modern classical style, designed by the famous architect Friedrich Schinkel. Gerson quickly expanded his business to include the sale of ready-made coats and capes. In 1848 Gerson, who by now owned an elegant three-storey department store on the *Werderschen Markt,*[6] was appointed supplier to the Prussian Royal household. Soon the name Herrmann Gerson signified highly exclusive and expensive ladies' fashions of international caliber in Berlin. By 1848 the firm employed, in addition to approximately 250 in-house employees, 1500 tailors, among them 150 master tailors, who produced clothing for the firm as

sub-contractors. In 1861 the House of Gerson was entrusted with creating the cape to be worn by Wilhelm I on the occasion of his coronation as King of Prussia. A decade later, when Wilhelm became German Emperor, the House of Gerson became the supplier for the Emperor's household. In 1889 Philipp Freudenberg, also Jewish, took over the business.[7] Early in 1938 the firm, having suffered severe losses in the economic crisis, was "Aryanized" (where ownership was forcibly trans-ferred from its Jewish owner to an "Aryan" nominee) by the fashion house Horn.[8]

The House Gerson was followed in 1837 by the opening of the House of the Brothers David, Moritz and Valentin Manheimer,[9] who produced ready-to-wear coats, and by Rudolph Hertzog[10] (1839) and David Leib Levin[11] (1840), who were among the first clothing businesses to work with fixed sale-prices.

The Berlin ready-to-wear trade, having gradually established itself in the neighborhood of the *Hausvogteiplatz,* became an important branch of the local economy as well as a growing

TOP LEFT: Receipt for garment order, Gerson, Berlin 1873.
SOURCE: C. Jahnke Collection

LEFT: Hand embroidered label from black velvet evening coat, late 1920s, Gerson.
SOURCE: C. Jahnke Collection

ABOVE: Illustration, masquerade costume, *Der Bazaar*, January, 1887. *Der Bazaar* was printed from 1855 to 1936. From 1877 the publisher was Leopold Ullstein, whose famous company was the largest in the world at the time. From 1912 the company also published *Die Dame* (The Lady), one of the most important fashion magazines in Germany in the twentieth century. The Ullsteins were originally orthodox Jews who converted to Lutheranism. Even so, the Nazis seized the publishing house and dismissed the family.

export business. Coats and capes, among other goods, became the leading items exported to Austria and England in 1857, and in the early 1860s to America, Scandinavia and Russia.[12] This extraordinary increase in the productive capacity of the ready-to-wear workshops resulted to no small extent from the introduction in 1851 of an improved and occupationally useful sewing machine by Isaac Merrit Singer.[13]

The professional training of a ready-to-wear planner or manager, who would now be referred to as a fashion designer, usually took place through an apprenticeship in a ready-to-wear factory, seldom under a master tailor.[14] Rarely did such a designer achieve personal fame. An exception to this was Kurt Ehrenfreund, who in 1933 had already emigrated to Amsterdam, where he founded a successful ready-to-wear establishment. His firm was Aryanized by the German occupation troops in 1940.[15]

THE DECADE OF ART NOUVEAU

Fashion at the turn of the century was defined by the so-called "Sans Ventre" style characteristic of art nouveau that reflected the idle lifestyle of an influential segment of society. These clothes were distinguished by stiff stand-up collars, very long sleeves, all-around floor-length material over frilly petticoats, and stiff S-shaped corsets. Paris alone was recognized as the prototype of fashion.

Pl. XII.
a.

BUREAUX ENCKEPLATZ 4. BERLIN.

DER BAZAR,
ILLUSTRIRTE DAMEN-ZEITUNG.
1. MAERZ, 1880.

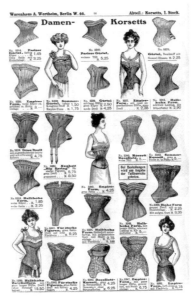

FACING PAGE: One dinner and two daytime ensembles, original fashion plage, *Der Bazaar,* March 1880.
SOURCE: C. Jahnke Collection

ABOVE: Corset, silk and satin stiffened with whalebone, B. Sonnenkalb, Hamburg, 1904.
PHOTO: Ernest von Rosen, AMG Media Works Inc.
SOURCE: C. Jahnke Collection

ABOVE RIGHT: Advertisement for corsets from Wertheim catalogue, 1903.
SOURCE: C. Jahnke Collection

The dependence on Paris was due not to a lack of creative ideas or fashion instinct among Berlin's fashion designers, but rather to customer demand. A mere suggestion of Parisian taste aroused the interest of customers. At the same time, fashion buyers from Berlin influenced the offerings of the Parisian couture houses, which valued the high demand for their creations from Berlin.

Recognizing the interest in Parisian fashion, houses such as Gerson, Manheimer and Israel maintained their own French departments in lavishly appointed salon rooms, where they offered original Parisian haute couture apparel for sale.[16] Of course, these houses also offered customers a made-to-measure department. Their customers included the Russian high aristocracy, the American Vanderbilts, and the Ducal House Thurn and Taxis, who ordered entire trousseaus to be assembled. Other customers included the wives of German bankers and leaders of industry such as Bertha Krupp, whose exquisite evening gowns were typical of the Wilhelmine era (1888-1918).

Clients of haute couture were drawn mainly from the bourgeois segment of the upper middle class, whose painstaking effort to be appropriately attired for every

LEFT: Fashion illustration by Mela Koehler for the Wiener Werkstätte, c. 1910.
SOURCE: C. Jahnke Collection

FACING PAGE: Afternoon dress, ivory cotton with yellow embroidery and braiding, label marked, "Hirsch & Cie, Modewaren Magasin, Hamburg, Reisendamm 2/3," c.1910. The dress was purchased at a vintage clothing sale in Toronto, Ontario, in 1991.
SOURCE: C. Jahnke Collection
PHOTO: Martin Tessler

Hirsch and Cie of Brussels, Amsterdam, Cologne, Dresden and Hamburg, was founded in 1869. M. Hirsch was decorated by the Queen of Belgium with the Order of Leopold. The house received gold medals at the National Exposition of Brussels in 1880, the International Exposition of Amsterdam in 1883, and the International Exposition of Antwerp in 1885.

occasion together with their wish to cultivate a distinctive look strongly stimulated business. In contrast consumers of the plain ready-to-wear, the so-called staple commodities (which could be compared with today's mass-produced clothing items), were members of the working class. Very promising in this genre was the "tricot-taillen." These were tops made of fine-meshed knitwear, considered an original Berlin fashion creation (though Viennese fashion designers claimed the "tricot-taille" as their original creation as well). The "tricot bodices" were exported even to the USA, where they were considered appropriate wear for "exchange ladies," the first telephone operators.

THE FIRST WORLD WAR

The First World War confronted German fashion designers with the significant challenge of demonstrating their independence from French fashion design and, at the same time, strengthening the German national fashion-consciousness. Elsa Herzog,[17] a leading columnist of the fashion journal *Elegante Welt*, wrote in March: "In 1915 Berlin is experiencing a new spring of fashion, an imposing event that forces German ready-to-wear manufacturers and tailors to proceed without the help of Parisian dress designs." In spite of this euphoria the First World

War brought a severe decline to the export business. Nineteen fifteen saw the founding of the Association of Ladies' Fashion and its Industry; among its members were both Jews and Christians.[18] German Jewish clothing manufacturers were extremely eager to emphasize their national consciousness.

In many combined fashion shows and exhibitions, fashion designers tried to showcase their creative independence and to attract export business for their goods. In 1917 during the Werkbund exhibition in Bern, the industry presented a lavish fashion show under the artistic direction of Otto Haas-Heye, who was granted a leave of absence from his military service for the occasion.

Otto Haas-Heye, who founded the famous Couture Salon Alfred-Marie in Berlin in December of 1914, was one of Germany's most artistic creators of fashion. The fashion press compared him to Paul Poiret but considered

FACING PAGE: Label from a formal afternoon dress, c. 1922 - 23. Heinrich Grünbaum's was one of the finest *haute couture* houses in Vienna, with shops in Vienna and in the spa town of Karlsbad (Karlovy Vary, Czech Republic). Grünbaum was in business from 1906 until 1936 when the store was Aryanized.
SOURCE: C. Jahnke Collection

LEFT: "Mannequin," afternoon dress by Johanna Marbach, *Styl* magazine, Berlin, 1922, Erich Reiss, publisher. The full title of this exclusive folio magazine, which was published for only two years, was, *Styl, Blätter für Mode und die angenehmen Dinge des Lebens.* (Style, Magazine for Fashion and the Pleasant Things of Life.)
SOURCE: C. Jahnke Collection

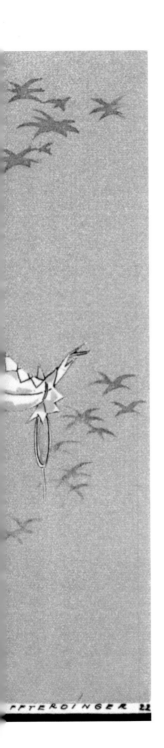

his creations to be too "fanciful" and therefore inappropriate for everyday life. Otto Haas-Heye, himself of Jewish ancestry, was a painter, esthete, and publisher. He permitted many of his creations to be sketched by the talented fashion artist Annie Offterdinger in highly collectible portfolios.[19] His fashionable line was distinguished by its refined, feminine elegance. His creations reflected the style of the modern "war-skirt" with its short, crinoline-shaped skirt. Despite all the nationalistic efforts, fashion still remained internationally consistent during the war years. Otto Haas-Heye closed his salon in 1917, most likely for reasons related to the war. In 1920, a department of fashion design opened at the School of the Museum of Applied Arts *(Unterrichtsanstalt des Kunstgewerbemuseums),* where Otto Haas-Heye was appointed as professor. He spent much of his time there as costume designer for the theatre.[20]

THE TWENTIES

High unemployment and steadily increasing inflation made the post World War I period one of great hardship. Only after 1924 did better times arrive. Berlin, which in 1925 had more than four million inhabitants, became the centre of artistic and intellectual life and the favored shopping destination, outranking even Paris and London.

Fashion became the expression of urban life. In 1924 fashion design achieved the typical silhouette of the twenties, with knee-length skirts and loose hanging dresses with waistlines resting low on the hips. The fashion of the day, with its straight "paletots," sporty knitted sweaters and narrow skirts, met the needs of ready-to-wear manufacturing. Graphic designs, in accordance with cubism and the new realism, provided fashion with its typical style; yet many Germans retained their taste for flower-printed fabrics.

The clientele had changed, however. The customer base for the clothing trade now consisted of young, lower middle-class women who as office workers had their first experience spending their own money. These young women wished to define their style as somewhere between a "business girl" during the day and a "seductive vamp" in the evening.

Stars of film and stage, together with the wives of war profiteers, formed the main clientele of the haute couture and made-to-measure departments. Their evening gowns had to be as extravagant as possible with very low necklines, soft chiffon or Georgette dresses with luxurious sequin-and-pearl embroidery

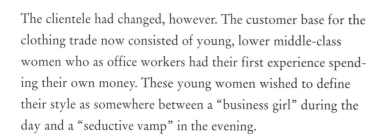

(so heavy that their narrow straps often broke under the weight), or velvet gowns with seams trimmed with monkey fur or ostrich feathers. Such exquisite fashions were purchased from the leading Jewish Salons: Glaser & Götz, Flatow & Schaedler, Gerson, Prager & Hausdorff, Kersten & Tuteur, Regina Friedländer, Hermann Hoffmann and Max Becker, as well as at the non-Jewish Johanna Marbach, Hilda Romatzki, and Marie Latz salons. Clientele were not interested in the ancestry or religion of the designers or the salon owners.

In this decade a high degree of creative independence was demanded of fashion designers, partially because Paris fashion design no longer exerted an all-powerful influence. Paris fashion now served solely as a means of "general orientation." Not only did customers travel to Berlin just to shop, but these buyers were also regular visitors to the "Fashion Weeks," regular cultural events held since 1917, becoming semi-annual clothing fairs in 1925. Buyers considered these programs of equal importance

to their real business – that of placing orders for new designs.

Berlin offered an abundance of entertainment, magnificent dance halls, and most importantly, extravagantly staged revues requiring an abundance of costumes. One of the most successful costume designers was Ernst Stern, of Jewish-Romanian origin,[21] who worked for many years for Max Reinhardt in Berlin and who, in the twenties, designed costumes for many Ernst Lubitsch[22] films and Erik Charell shows.[23] While these outfits were mostly fantastic creations, the actors in plays and operettas were actually dressed in current fashions rather than theatrical costumes. It was the custom of the trade to name the fashion house entrusted with dressing the actors in the program notes. The stars of the stage, many of whom left Germany in the thirties, also functioned as mannequins (models). Among them were Fritzi Massary,[24] Tilla Durieux, Asta Nielsen and finally, Marlene Dietrich. Fritzi Massary, who obtained her stage costumes as well as her private fashions exclusively from the House Clara Schultz,[25] was admired as one of the most elegantly attired stars of this period.

FACING PAGE: Actress Fritzi
Massary.

CENTRE: Exhibition of women's
fashion, held in Kaiserdamm
1927.
SOURCE: AKG

ABOVE RIGHT: Cover, *Elegante
Welt*, No. 23, 1921.
SOURCE: C. Jahnke Collection

Fashion shows were now produced in the style of a theatre performance or as a fashion revue, with the gowns modeled by celebrated stars. This practice was intended to showcase the international quality of the fashions of Berlin and thus stimulate export of these goods.

The most influential German fashion journals *Elegante Welt* (Elegant World) and *Die Dame* (The Lady), both founded in 1912, introduced the creations of the German fashion salons in the same manner as they used in reporting the Paris fashion scene. Elsa Herzog and Ola Alsen, both Jewish,[26] were leading fashion journalists as was Lieselotte Friedländer,[27] also Jewish, a fashion graphic artist for *Moden Spiegel* (Mirror of Fashion) first published in 1922. The regrettably short-lived journal *Styl* (Style), published by the Association of Ladies' Fashions and Industry, survived only from 1922 to 1924. This journal

"Hello" was the nickname of Helene Wolff Budischowsky. At one time "Hello" was married to Fritz Wolff, the owner of the Knize tailoring firm. Ernst Dryden designed clothing for both businesses.

After 1938, "Hello" re-opened in London. Ernst Dryden became a designer of fashion and movie costumes in Hollywood, California. His work appeared in such films as *The Garden of Allah* with Marlene Dietrich (1936), *The Lady of Athens* (1937), *Lost Horizon* (1937), *The King Steps Out* (1937) and *Doctor Rhythm* (1938).

FACING PAGE: Hello storefront in Vienna.

ABOVE: Label for man's tuxedo suit, black wool and silk, label marked, "Knizé; Paris, Berlin, Wien, Karlsbad," dated 1934. SOURCE: C. Jahnke Collection

LEFT: Fashion drawing by Ernst Dryden for Knizé, c. 1928. Knizé was founded in Vienna by a Czech family in 1858 and purchased in 1880 by Albert Wolff, a Berlin Jew. Under his direction, and with the talented designs of Ernst Dryden, the company became one of the finest tailoring houses in Europe. "A suit from Knizé was the fantasy of a generation of young Austrians." (Anthony Lipmann, *Divinely Elegant*, 1989).

FACING PAGE: Woman's evening dress, black silk velvet, unlabelled, Vienna, c. 1935 - 38.
SOURCE: C. Jahnke Collection
PHOTO: Martin Tessler

LEFT: Cover, *Elegante Welt*, No. 3, 1930.
SOURCE: C. Jahnke Collection

contained sketches by Annie Offterdinger[28] and Ludwig Kainer, whose elevated artistic standard placed them among the top rank of fashion artists in the world.

THE THIRTIES

During the thirties fashion returned to a very feminine line that accentuated the female body, charmingly sporty during the day and elegantly ladylike for eveningwear. The new calf-length hem together with broad shoulders, as launched by Elsa Schiaparelli in 1931, found general acceptance.[29]

In National Socialist (Nazi) Germany, the fashion scene, as well as the political culture as a whole, expressed the ambivalence between an imaginary ideal and reality, between wish and actuality, between ideology and economy. It was the goal of "official" fashion ventures, together with the party-loyal fashion journals, to launch a "German Fashion." The majority of creative fashion designers, both Jewish and non-Jewish, and publishers of respected fashion magazines were equally determined to initiate a world-class, urban, elegant fashion industry. The creative uncertainty of the period led many fashion designers, even more than in the twenties, to adopt Paris as their guide to fashion. However, a difference in style

between Jewish and non-Jewish fashion houses did not exist. Both groups were more or less guided by their own independent creativity.

An example of these ambivalent endeavors is provided by the *Deutsches Modeamt* (German Fashion Institute) founded in Berlin in June 1933 with the cooperation of the *Reichsminister für Volksaufklärung und Propaganda* (Peoples' Enlightenment and Propaganda). German fashion creations were introduced in regularly scheduled fashion shows, which were timed to coincide with fashion shows opening in Paris. The first of these events, in August of 1933, attracted 150 fashion creators.[30] Among those participating were nearly all of the old, established salons, including the Jewish House Max Becker.[31] The next show in October 1933, under the auspices of the *Deutsches Mode-Institut*, the renamed *Modeamt*, was attended by Hermann Hoffman, whose Jewish clothing business was Aryanized in 1938. Hoffman won an honorable mention at this show for his excellent sporty fashion.[32]

In 1934 the journal *Die Dame*[33] published a photo of an original dress design from the renowned House Gerson, as well as an ensemble created by another Jewish House, the House Strassner.

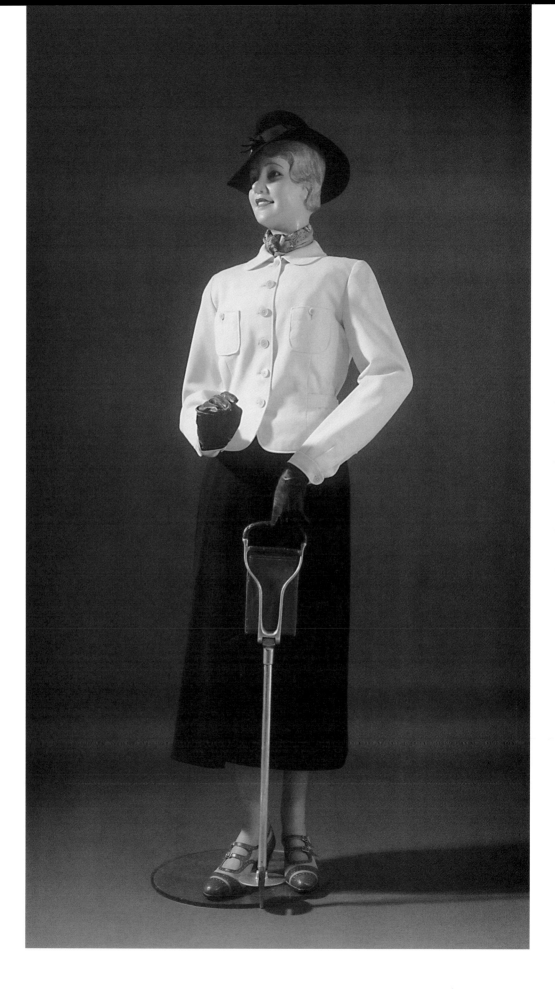

DIE *Dame*

PFERDE *und* REITER

DEUTSCHER VERLAG BERLIN

The Silberspiegel (Silver Mirror) praised the effect, achieved
through the innovative use of colour and fabric, of these sporty,
simple dresses, and the *Elegante Welt*[34] stated: "the German
Fashion Institute has, for the second time, helped German
Fashion to succeed – the distinguished models reflect the
German woman in the framework of worldwide fashions." *Die
Schöne Frau* (The Beautiful Woman), a journal loyal to the Nazi
regime, complained that the work of the *Deutsches Mode-Institut*
failed to reflect the spirit of National Socialism.[35] Famous

FACING PAGE: Cover, *Die Dame,* 1938.
SOURCE: C. Jahnke Collection

fashion houses, including the House of Harald Mahrenholz, who emigrated to London in 1937, the new House Schulze-Bibernell, as well as the House Gerson, which was Aryanized in 1937 through the firm Horn, also participated in the 1936 fashion show. No stylistic difference between the fashion creations of Jewish and non-Jewish fashion Houses existed; there were just talented and less-talented designers. Most fashion creators and manufacturers continued to visit Paris, not always legally due to the shortage of foreign exchange.

Heinz Schulze, whose refined patterns and drapes were much admired, was one of the most creative independent fashion designers. Apprenticed in the House Gerson, Heinz Schulze was soon employed as a fashion designer by Norbert Jutschenka. Schulze declined Jutschenka's offer to take over his business during the Nazi Aryanization drive, instead opening an independent shop in 1934. He always found ways of declining work for the ladies of the Nazi regime. In 1943 he was offered the post of chief of the UFA film company's costume crew. He declined to swear the oath to the Führer, a necessary condition of UFA employment and chose military service instead.[36]

In 1943 all fashion magazines were required to cease publication as conditions worsened during the war. This edict applied even to the lavishly produced journal, *Die Mode* (The Fashion), which only began publishing in 1941, despite its loyalty to the Nazi regime.

There is little doubt that, as Magda Goebbels remarked: "Along with the Jews, elegance disappeared from Berlin." This was brought about not only by the disappearance from the scene of the Jewish fashion creators, but also through the loss of the many elegant Jewish customers who bought their clothing in Berlin.

ABOVE: Label from man's cutaway tail coat, black wool and silk satin, pre 1938.
SOURCE: C. Jahnke Collection

FACING PAGE: Cover, *Die Dame,* September 1933. Designed by Ernst Dryden.
SOURCE: C. Jahnke Collection

Following the annexation of Austria to the German Reich in March of 1938, it was hoped that Vienna would be elevated to the rank of the "Reich's Capital City of Fashion." In contrast to Berlin, with its large department stores, fashion in Vienna was characterized by individual salons, which explored the taste of their customers and adapted Parisian fashion to the tastes of the Viennese.

ENDNOTES

1 Following the "Jew Edict" promulgated on May 21, 1671, by Friedrich Wilhelm, Grand Duke of Brandenburg (1640-1688), Jews were permitted to deal in old and new clothes. These "illegal" tailors, including many Jews, were known as "Pfuscher" (bunglers) or "Störer" (disturbers). (See Uwe Westphal, *Ready-to-Wear and Fashion in Berlin 1836-1939: The Destruction of a Tradition*. Berlin 1986. Gretel Wagner, "Fashion in Berlin" in *Berlin en vogue: Berlin Fashion in Photography*. edited by F.C. Grundlach und Uli Richter. Berlin, 1993.)

2 During that time many Hugenots, who were very competent craftsmen, having been expelled from France (Edict of Potsdam, 1635) later worked as tailors in Prussia.

3 Uniform tailors took pride in their cutting style, accurate work and prompt delivery.

4 The German word "Konfektion" is derived from the Latin "conficere," meaning "to make ready" or "prepare."

5 Herrmann Gerson, actually Hirsch Gerson Levin, came to Berlin in 1835. After his death his brothers continued to manage the business until it was taken over (initially as a partner) by Philipp Freudenberg in 1889.

6 The House Gerson grew continually larger, so that the complex covered several streets. There were always new buildings or reconstructions of old ones. The final rebuilding of the business (1921-1922) was directed by the well-known architect Hermann Muthesius.

7 Philipp Freudenberg founded a department store in his hometown in 1863 and gained valuable experience in the management of a modern store. In 1888 he relocated to Berlin. Following his death his brothers assumed the management of the House Gerson. In the twenties this House served stars of film and theatre. The merged fashion firms of Gerson, Prager and Hausdorff, situated in the Bellevue Street area of Berlin, created highly original fashion designs.

8 The firms of Herrmann Gerson and Kersten & Tuteur were taken over by the still-existing Fashion House Horn, located on the Kurfürstendamm in Berlin.

9 In 1839 Valentin Manheimer opened his own business, which in 1929, under the management of his grandson Adolph Manheimer, suffered extensive losses and had to be sold. The Brothers Manheimer business is entered in the record of Berlin fashion houses for the last time in 1932.

10 The Christian clothing manufacturing and department store of Rudolph Hertzog remained under the ownership of the founding family and was the only clothing manufacturing business to survive the Nationalist Socialist regime.

11 The ladies' and children's fashion house D. Levin survived into the twenties.

12 In 1875 the turnover of Berlin's ready-to-wear industry totaled 22.5 million Reichsmarks. Four million was earned by exports to the USA and Canada, three million from exports to England, and one million from exports to Holland and Switzerland. (Brunhilde Dähn, *Berlin Hausvogteiplatz*. Göttingen, 1968, p. 51).

13 An automatic buttonhole machine was patented in 1862, and a machine for sewing on buttons in 1875.

14 Tailors received their training during an apprenticeship in a suitable shop followed by a master's test set by their guild. 1862 saw the founding of the Hirsch Academy of Tailoring, which was the first school to train a new generation of tailors for the clothing industry. The trade journal *Der Konfektionär* was first published in 1886.

15 Kurt Ehrenfreund went underground shortly before his deportation. He founded a new clothing factory in Amsterdam in 1945. In 1952 he emigrated to the USA.

16 In 1911 the celebrated Paris fashion designer Paul Poiret was invited by the fashion house Gerson to show his new collection in Berlin. Poiret's designs were based on the fashion style of the empire. The Reform Dress design was more successful in Berlin than in Paris in part because the simply-cut dresses and tunics were ideally suited for production of ready-to-wear.

17 See note #26.

18 Herman Freudenberg, brother of Philipp Freudenberg, was the first chairman. (See note #7). Adelheid Rasche, Peter Jessen, The Berlin Society of Fashion Museums and the Association of the German Fashion Industry, 1916 to 1925, in *Magazine of the Society of Historic Weapons and Costume*, Vol. 37, 1995, p. 74ff.

19 It is not known whether Annie Offterdinger was of Jewish descent. In the twenties she worked as a fashion journalist in Paris. After 1931 she frequently changed her residence until her emigration to the USA in 1936. Efforts by Sabine Runde, author of "Welt ohne Alltag. Modegraphik der 20er Jahre von Annie Offterdinger," Museum für Kunsthandwerk,

Frankfurt am Main, 1986, to find information about her have been fruitless. Her date of death remains unknown. A total of eight folios of her work can be found in German art and fashion libraries.

20 Otto Haas-Heye went to Paris in 1926 as an art advisor. He lived in Zurich from 1930 to 1936 and founded the Art and Fashion School of Zurich. In 1938 he briefly returned to Berlin, only to emigrate to London in the same year where he remained in London until 1958. (Gretel Wagner, "Otto Haas-Heye: Die Zeit in Berlin," 1914–1925, unpublished).

21 Ernst Stern studied at the Munich Academy of Arts under the famous painter Franz Stuck. Since Stern lived abroad in 1933 for professional reasons, he returned to Germany only to bring his wife and daughter abroad. He was not allowed to take any money with him out of Germany. Stern had already made valuable contacts in London and was able to continue outfitting operettas and films. Stern became a German citizen in 1921, awarded by the Weimar Republic. It was revoked by the Nazi regime.

22 The film director Ernst Lubitsch was the son of a well-known clothing manufacturer. Lubitsch emigrated to the USA for professional reasons in 1922.

23 Erik Charell's successes included the globally acclaimed operetta "Im Weissen Rössl" by Ralph Benatzky, performed under the title "The White Horse Inn" in London (1931) and in New York (1936).

24 Fritzi Massary arrived in Berlin in 1904 and emigrated to the USA in 1933.

25 The Salon of Clara Schultz had existed since 1900 and, for unknown reasons, was converted to a public company in 1934.

26 Elsa Herzog was forced to emigrate to London in 1939. After the end of the war she resumed her work for the journal *Elegante Welt*. In 1958 she was awarded the Service Cross of the German Republic. (Gretel Wagner, "Fashion in Berlin" in *Berlin en vogue: Berlin Fashion in Photography*, edited by F.C. Grundlach und Uli Richter, Berlin 1993, p. 120). Ola Alsen emigrated during the thirties.

27 Lieselotte Friedländer had her permission to work revoked in 1933 because she was a quarter Jew. Thereafter, she worked under false names and later lived in the countryside under her mother's maiden name. In 1949 she returned to Berlin but failed to secure worthwhile commissions. (Christa Gustavus, "Lieselotte Friedländer and the *Moden-Spiegel*," in *Fashion in the Twenties*. Catalogue of the Berlin Museum, Berlin 1991, p. 38).

28 See note #19.

29 Elsa Schiaparelli was inspired by the broad shoulders of the British Guardsmen as well as by the Pagoda shoulders of Thai dancers.

30 The fashion salons are not named, but can be identified on the basis of the photographs of models. (Gretel Wagner, "Das Deutsche Mode-Institut 1933-1941," in *Zeitschrift der Gesellschaft für Historische Waffen-und Kostümkunde*, 1997, p. 85.)

31 The fashion House Max Becker can be traced up to the mid 1930s. According to witnesses the owners emigrated to London. (Gretel Wagner, p. 126).

32 *Der Konfektionär*, 1934, Vol. 9, p. 10.

33 *Die Dame*, 1934, Vol. 7, pp. 21-22.

34 *Elegante Welt*, 1934, Vol. 6, p. 10.
Der Silberspiegel, Die Neue Linie as well as *Die Dame* were all compelled to cease publication in 1943. The editor-in-chief of *Die Dame*, Kurt Korff, had been forced to leave Germany earlier. During the thirties the editor-in-chief of *Elegante Welt*, F.W. Koebner, was forced to relinquish control to the Staff Officer Hubert Miketta. F.W. Koebner revived *Elegante Welt* in Stuttgart in 1949. The journal ceased publication in 1969.

35 For this reason the former director of the German Fashion Institute, Dr. Hans Horst, was replaced in 1934 by Dr. Herbert Tengelmann, who played a decisive role in the Aryanization of the Institute of Industry and Trade. In 1936 the moderate, but professionally competent fashion journalist Hela Strehl was appointed to the post of director. (Gretel Wagner, p. 89).

36 Heinz Schulze opened a fashion salon in Munich in 1947 under the name of Heinz Schulze-Varell.

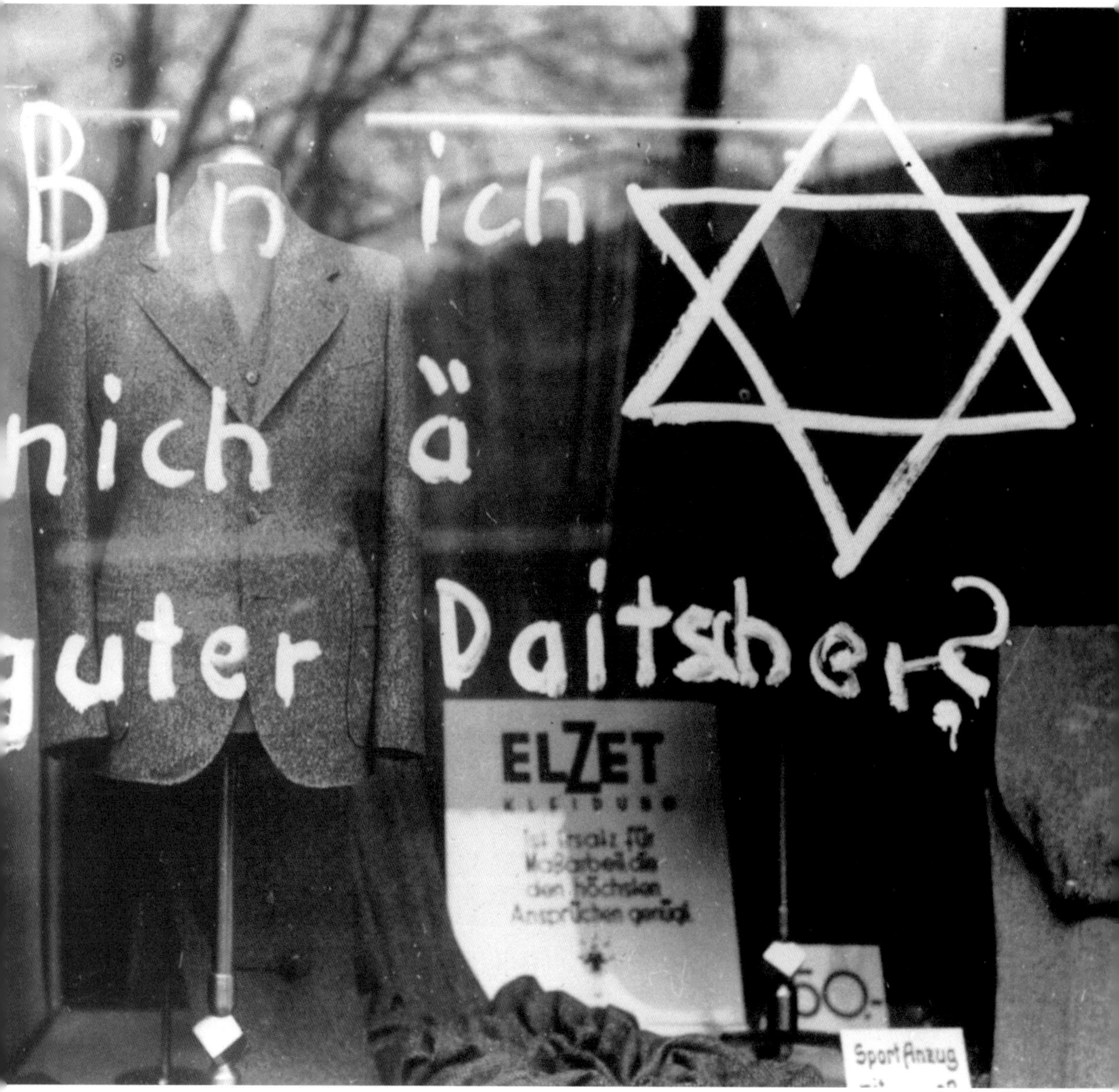
Bin ich
nich ä
guter Daitscher?
ELZET
60.-
Sport Anzug

The Destruction of a Culture and an Industry

Irene Guenther

For centuries, Germany viewed France as its biggest fashion competitor, culturally and economically.[1]

Already in the 1600s, German poems and satirical picture sheets circulated that railed against foreign, particularly French, fashion foes. Throughout the 18th and 19th centuries, innumerable articles and essays conveyed the fear that the increased popularity of "licentious" French fashions in Germany threatened the nation's "more virtuous" Nordic society. These cultural contestations escalated, first, during the Napoleonic occupation of German territories and, then again, after the Franco-Prussian War of 1870-71 and the founding of the Second German Empire. In the realm of fashion, Germany profited from France's resounding defeat and ensuing civil upheaval. Berlin's ready-to-wear exports totaled 10 million marks annually while Paris was engulfed in internal strife. Markedly heightening the French-German vitriol and rivalry in the opening years of the 20th century, Kaiser Wilhelm voiced his disdain for French culture by calling Paris "the great whorehouse of the world." Equally colorful French condemnations decried a German "alien influence" that intended to "insidiously subvert" French culture and, ultimately, France itself.

The Nazi Party's platform claimed to be committed to dissolving department stores to help small businesses. In reality, they wanted to eliminate Jewish ownership. Only Jews were forced to sell, mostly far below true value.

Nazis targeted Jewish department stores as agents of modernism – capitalism, socialism, republicanism and urbanism – as opposed to 'traditional' German values. This propaganda increased hostility among smaller merchants who could not compete.

Nazi propaganda instilled the notion that department stores were all Jewish-owned. Although all but three (Karstadt, Kaufhof and R. Herzog) of the major Berlin department stores were owned by Jewish merchants, there were also many successful non-Jewish-owned department stores in Germany.

The onset of World War I in August 1914 further inflamed cultural hostilities. The German fashion industry viewed the war as providing the perfect opportunity to persuade German women that German fashion was far superior to the "tasteless, immoral" fashions created by France. Monetary profits were not the only issue at stake. Intertwined with economic factors were rampant nationalism and cultural preeminence. The goals were to attain complete independence from French influence, to develop a uniquely German fashion that would sell well within the nation and abroad, and to inhabit the preeminent position in the international fashion scene traditionally occupied by Paris. A wartime ban on French fashion terms was imposed. Shopkeepers had to clear their shelves of French perfumes. And, published editorials questioned the depth of women's patriotism when they persisted in wearing French fashions while their men were being "murdered" by the brutal French enemy.

Still in the 1920s, critics bitterly deplored the "decadent" French influence on German clothes. They also insisted that French fashions were unhealthy for German women, morally and phys- ically. Clearly, the war had encouraged, but did not resolve, the contentious competitiveness that had long characterized French- German relations in the realm of fashion.

The war also exacerbated anti-Semitism, which had surfaced occasionally and, at times, virulently in the pre-war years. Soon after the conflict began, lectures and essays appeared that inveighed against the Jews for undermining German culture, for shirking their military duty, and for making huge sums of money from the slaughter. Conservative critics linked Jews with modernists as symbolic of all that was considered degenerate in contemporary society and culture. Moreover, by the early 20th century, Jews had become notable economic successes in Germany, both as proprietors of large department stores and as prominent leaders in the garment industry. Profitable before

ABOVE: "Jew" written on the windows of a Jewish-owned clothing store. Photograph taken during boycotts of April 1933.
SOURCE: Yad Vashem Archives, Jerusalem, Israel.

World War I, Berlin's *Hausvogteiplatz* became an international fashion center in the postwar years. It was particularly known for ready-to-wear apparel; Jews were predominant in that branch of the industry. Their success was used against them by anti-Semites who resented the Jews' visibility and prosperity.

Especially as the young Weimar Republic convulsed from the economic chaos brought on by unprecedented inflation and political instability, critics manipulated facts to justify their claims that Jews had "taken over" the German clothing industry through "unscrupulous," "un-German" business dealings. They were, thereby, ruining economic opportunities for the German middle class. Because of this supposed "stranglehold," Jews also had the power to contaminate fashions and, there-with, German women. Even after the nation had stabilized, right-wing conservatives argued that German women were becoming immoral because of "impudent" and "insolent" fashions, provably initiated by "Jewish racketeers." Such "hideous" clothes, a "satanic mockery of womanhood," epitomized "the stylized costume of the city whore, a specific Jewish invention." One author warned that the once noble image of the German woman was descending into the depths of depravity, and that the Jews were at the helm of this

People who shop in Jewish-owned stores are singled out for humiliation. Non-Jewish customers entering Jewish stores are pho-tographed. Their names and pictures are published in the local press or displayed on billboards. Each is considered "a traitor to his people."

conspiracy: "Powers are at work to destroy feminine dignity.
They are sworn to annihilate the Aryan race which is chastely
conscious of its human dignity."

Although their position in the clothing industry never amounted
to the "80-90% Jewish takeover" cited by anti-Semitic agitators,
by the end of the 1920s German Jews owned several of Berlin's
largest department stores and controlled approximately 49
percent of clothing design and manufacturing. Such visible
accomplishments made them easy scapegoats in the inflammatory
Depression climate of the early 1930s. Once the Nazis came to
power, all of the various strands of the age-old fashion dispute
crystallized into one argument: Only German fashion, Aryan-
designed and manufactured, was appropriate for the "noble
German woman." Racially-correct German clothing depended
upon the elimination of Jewish and French influences. An early
1933 article summarized this view:

> We know...that the Parisian whores set the tone for
> the fashions offered to German women, yes that...
> Jewish Konfektion dealers and designers concoct
> 'high' fashion in cahoots with the spinning and
> weaving industries, and with the help of the whore

*world that parades their wares....Shame and disgrace,
degradation and debasement of German taste, of
German self-reliance.... Should this nightmare never
end?....Now under the signs of the swastika, the*
Wendekreuz, *the sun wheel....It is time that the
German brotherhood within the new all-encompassing
state begins to stir in the hearts of fashion-conscious
German shoppers. Or else the all-embracing state will
have to resort to force in the realm of taste as well.*

Now the opportunity presented itself to silence Germany's
trendsetting French neighbor, to banish the "poisonous" Jewish
presence, to rid the nation of the "spiritual [fashion] cocaine"
produced by "Jewish masterminds," and to create a "purely
German fashion." To that end, "French" and "Jewish" were
often co-mingled in the virulent propaganda; however, Jews
became the focus of the fashion industry purge. Nazi stalwarts,
who saw monetary opportunities coupled with state-sponsored
anti-Semitism, jumped at the chance to rid the nation's economy

of its Jewish participants. Only six years after the Nazi Party came to power, these long-held prejudices, now officially sanctioned, brought about irreparable economic damage, irretrievable cultural dispossession, and grievous human loss.

On April 1, 1933, a boycott against the Jews began. It was not the first time this type of action had been launched against Germany's Jews. Throughout the 1920s, but especially during the worst Depression years, 1929-1932, numerous voluntary boycotts and individual cases of violence against Jews had occurred. These were usually instigated by extreme right-wing groups. The April 1 state-organized boycott was justified as a "defensive measure" against Jewish "atrocity propaganda." However, its obvious intent was to force Jews out of the economy in favor of their non-Jewish German competitors. SA and Hitler Youth members were stationed outside of Jewish-owned small retail shops, larger department stores, and professional offices. They were armed with anti-Semitic posters and, occasionally, with cameras to take pictures of non-Jews who, in spite of the boycott, frequented Jewish establishments. Public harassment and intermittent violence occurred. The Nazi-initiated boycott officially lasted one day, but continued unofficially in varying degrees.

Dr. Michael Siegal, an eminent Jewish lawyer, lodged a complaint with the Munich police after the windows of a Jewish-owned store, *Kaufhaus Uhlfedler*, had been smashed in March 1933. Nazi stormtroopers beat him at police headquarters, knocking out his front teeth and perforating his eardrum. His trouser legs cut off, Dr. Siegal was then marched through the streets of Munich wearing this placard: "I am a Jew, but I will never again complain about the Nazis."
SOURCE: Hulton Deutsche Collection Ltd., London

FACING PAGE: A crowd in front of a Jewish-owned department store in Berlin on April 1, 1933, the first day of the boycott. Signs urging Germans not to buy from Jews are posted on the storefront.
SOURCE: USHMM Archives

Aryanization the "transfer" of Jewish businesses to non-Jewish, Aryan ownership and the liquidation of Jewish businesses were alternative tactics employed by anti-Semites. All were accomplished through the use of intense pressure, distasteful methods, and highly suspect legal means. The April 1 boycott is important in that it paved the way for the step-by-step exclusion of Jews from the nation's economy, one of the Nazis' primary goals. Moreover, the state-sanctioned boycott legitimized any future organized or spontaneous actions that furthered this objective.

On May 4, 1933, at the invitation of Georg Riegel, an early Nazi pioneer and a long-established clothier in *Konfektion* (ready-to-wear), fifty men met at the Berliner Ratskeller. Their aim was to establish an organization whose objectives were to create a purely German *Konfektion* and to find work for jobless Germans in the fashion industry. At first, the group called itself the Federation of German Manufacturers of the Clothing Industry.[2] Within a year, however, the organization officially registered a telling change to its name. Henceforth, it was the Federation of German-Aryan Manufacturers of the Clothing Industry,[3] better known as Adefa. Its publicly-stated goals paralleled the ominous insertion of "Aryan" into its original name. These included breaking the Jewish "monopoly" in the

German clothing industry and "permanently eradicating" Jewish persons and Jewish influence in the "design, production, and sale" of German clothing and textiles. According to a contemporary newspaper article, these "fifty brave men," fueled with little money but with much idealism and a fighting spirit, began to "chisel away at the dangerously ubiquitous Jewish influence" in the German fashion industry.

In January 1934, only eight months after Adefa's founding, its director announced that an ongoing exhibition of wide-ranging fashion items produced by Adefa-member firms "gave proof that the monopoly of non-Aryans in the clothing industry had been broken." Further, the exhibit "provided tangible evidence" that the ready-to-wear branch of the clothing industry had been "successfully permeated with National Socialism's economic outlook." This glowing report, however, was not quite accurate.

While it was true that German Jews were being forced out of the fashion industry, this was not occurring as quickly as Adefa's leadership had predicted. In rural areas, because of the lack of competition, it had been relatively easy to ostracize Jews from the garment and retail trades. However, in large cities like Berlin, business ties were strong and long-standing between

> "Elegance will now disappear from Berlin along with the Jews."
>
> Magda Goebbels, wife of Joseph Goebbels, Nazi Minister of Propaganda, 1938

well-established German and German-Jewish suppliers, designers, and manufacturers. Likewise, urban consumers either looked for the best values being offered or continued purchasing from their favorite department stores and fashion salons, regardless of the barrage of false accusations hurled at "noxious Jewish parasites" in the clothing industry. Even the wives of highly-placed Nazi officials, like Magda Goebbels or Emmy Göring, persisted in frequenting their favorite Jewish designers. In fact, the secret *Sicherheitsdienst* morale report of April 1936 noted, "Party comrades and non-Party citizens alike continue, sometimes even while in uniform, to not shy away from making their purchases at Jewish establishments."

Still in 1937, the executive director of Adefa complained that "numbers of irresponsible retailers are purchasing approximately forty million *Reichsmarks* worth of clothing goods annually from Jewish wholesalers, and then passing these on to an unknowing, unsuspecting public." According to his calculations, "fourteen million Germans are still being clothed by the Jew today." His unsubstantiated jeremiad was published in several leading German newspapers. It was clear that something drastic had to be done. Beginning in late 1937, activities aimed at ousting the Jews from Germany's clothing industry noticeably increased.

FACING PAGE: "German clothing instead of Jewish *Konfektion*" reads the headline in the 1938 German publication *Arbeit und Wahr* (Work and Defense). At the end of 1939, the Nazis Aryanized the Berlin *Konfektion* industry.
SOURCE: *Berliner Konfektion und Mode* by Uwe Westphal, 1986.

BELOW: From *The Daily Colonist*, Victoria, BC, June 16, 1938.

Buying From Jews Ground for Divorce In German Courts

BERLIN, June 15 (CP-Havas). — Buying in a Jewish store is legitimate ground for divorce in German courts, a Nazi legal review revealed today. It reported a case in which a husband sued for divorce on charges that his wife had purchased from Jewish shopkeepers despite his express ban.

Das Zeichen für ADEFA Ware aus arischer Hand

Deutsche Kleidung statt jüdischer Konfektion

«Deutsche Kleidung statt jüdischer Konfektion», so lautet die Überschrift zu dem Artikel in der Zeitschrift (über)
und Wehr) von 1938. Am Ende des Jahres, nach dem November-Pogrom, hatten die Nationalsozialisten die
Berliner Konfektion «arisiert».

At the Adefa meeting of November 15, 1937, members agreed upon resolutions that would help bring to fruition the "speedy elimination of Jews from all branches of the garment industry." Several of these directives made mandatory what had been voluntary. Signs had to be displayed in Adefa-member shop windows, which would inform the public that only products "made by Aryan hands" were sold there.[4] Additionally, Adefa labels had to be sewn into all clothing items produced by the group's members, in order to "reassure our German comrades that every stage – from the weaver of the material to the producer of the clothing – was accomplished solely by Aryans." Before, the Adefa emblem had been utilized primarily in the men's and women's outerwear branches. Now, manufacturers of related products, such as underclothing and lingerie, ties, hats, work clothes, and umbrellas, were also directed to use the label. Finally, all members were forbidden from having future business

FACING PAGE: Lounging pajamas, black and white rayon satin, label marked *ADEFA, Arbeitsgemeinschaft deutsch-arischer Fabrikanten der Bekleidungsindustrie, e.V., Deutsches Erzeugnis,* Berlin, c. 1936. Purchased in a vintage clothing store, Toronto, Ontario, 1993.
SOURCE: C. Jahnke Collection
PHOTO: Martin Tessler

BELOW: These Adefa labels in German clothing assured the buyer that the garment was manufactured "by Aryan hands only."

dealings with Jews. For this stipulation to have been deemed necessary four years after Adefa was founded, it must have been painfully obvious that at least some of the group's members had maintained their ties with Jews. A new slogan to accompany this concerted effort to "finally cleanse" the fashion industry of remaining Jews was announced at the large two-day Adefa fashion exhibit in January 1938. The motto "We can do it better!" was repeated countless times to convince German consumers that Aryans were more capable than Jews of producing high-quality fashion items.[5]

On January 20, 1938, a new organization, known as Adebe, was founded to broaden the scope of these purification efforts. Its goals were to cultivate and safeguard National Socialist ideals in the textile, clothing, and leather industries; to eliminate all business ties between German and Jewish enterprises connected with these industries; to support and promote German businesses involved in these industries; and to help create a German "clothing culture." Many of the men who held leading positions in Adefa were also deeply involved in Adebe, and both groups shared similar objectives. Essentially, the addition of Adebe to the anti-Semitic agenda of Adefa simply widened the web of activities aimed at eliminating Jews from all aspects of the German clothing industry. Less than six months later, the web widened further. On June 4, 1938, forty influential members of Arwa, an association of cap manufacturers and suppliers, voted to merge Arwa into Adefa.[7] Additionally, they resolved to use the "Aryan-made" Adefa emblem on all of their products and to implement the Adefa resolutions of November 1937 in their business practices.

At the July 4, 1938 meeting, Adefa, officials announced that because "the Jewish problem has almost completely been dealt with, it is time to fulfill our cultural-political tasks." These included creating a "German clothing culture free from foreign influence" and "assisting in the creation of purely and uniquely German fashion masterpieces for domestic and foreign markets." Further, attending members were told that Aryanizations and, especially, closings and liquidations of Jewish clothing enterprises were proceeding at an accelerated rate. The envied and resented age-old Jewish presence in Germany's large and profitable fashion industry was coming to an end.

On November 9 and 10, 1938, Kristallnacht unfolded, a pogrom that unleashed fury and violence on all remaining Jewish shops, synagogues, and homes. Alongside the destruction of property,

more than twenty-five thousand Jewish men were arrested and put into concentration camps. Although the Nazi government termed the pogrom a "spontaneous public action," it was state orchestrated; Propaganda Chief Goebbels, the SA, and the SS were all involved. Two days later, on November 12, the Ordinance on the Exclusion of Jews from German Economic Life was enacted.[8] It hardly seemed necessary.

At the grand Adefa-organized fashion show in early January 1939, the group's leadership announced several new tasks since "Adefa's initial objective of excluding the Jews has been reached." The most important goal was to "extirpate all memories of Jewish methods, of Jewish sales techniques, and of the Jewish spirit." A dire warning ensued, "So long as the Jewish spirit in every sense and form is not banished from the clothing industry, the danger remains that Jewish parasites will again find entrance

into the German clothing industry." The district economic
adviser and Nazi official deeply involved in the Aryanization of
Jews from the fashion industry, Otto Jung, then reported that
almost two hundred additional Jewish firms in the women's and
men's branches of the clothing industry had been forced to close
their shops by the end of 1938. "Only five Jewish firms," he
proclaimed, "have not yet taken the leap into liquidation!"

Kristallnacht, November 9-10, 1938.
SOURCE: Wiener Library, London

"I have seen several anti-Jewish outbreaks in Germany during the last five years, but never anything as nauseating as this. Racial hatred and hysteria seemed to have taken complete hold of otherwise decent people."

Hugh Carleton Green
Berlin correspondent, *London Daily Telegraph*
November 10, 1938

Kristallnacht

German for "Night of Broken Glass." After the anti-Semitic riots on November 9, 1938, the streets of Germany and Austria were filled with broken glass from the windows of synagogues, homes and Jewish shops that had been destroyed.

The destruction of Nathan Israel's department store was the sacking of a Berlin institution. Founded in 1815, it was the first and oldest Jewish-owned department store. On November 9, 1938, Kurt Liepart, a buyer in the carpet department, warned Israel not to open the next day. However, the Israels, who had highly placed friends in the police, believed they would be protected. The store had armed guards until afternoon, when they mysteriously disappeared and the looting began. The SS rounded up as many of the Jewish staff as they could.

In Germany, 7,500 stores and 29 warehouses were destroyed, 267 synagogues were razed by fire, 76 more smashed, 171 houses destroyed, 11 community centres and similar buildings torched, another 3 gutted, and at least 30,000 Jewish men – many injured – were arrested and thrown into concentration camps. In Vienna, over 4,000 Jewish businesses were looted and 2,000 Jewish homes were Aryanized. Many people were injured, some were killed.

Following Kristallnacht, a fine of 1 billion marks (worth about $400 million at that time) was levied against the Jewish community for damages caused by the Nazi Party rioters. Göring's order of April 27, 1938, required the registration of all Jewish holdings. The Nazis could thus tabulate the atonement fine at 15% of the exact dollar value of all registered Jewish property.

On August 15, 1939, two weeks before the Second World War commenced, a packed membership assembly was told that Adefa had fulfilled all of its aims. It had conquered the "98% Jewish domination" in *Konfektion*. Adefa had severed all ties between Jewish and German suppliers, manufacturers, and owners. And, it had cleaned up the center of the ready-to-wear industry, Berlin's *Hauptvogteiplatz*, the "gathering point of Jewish corruption." The organization was then declared "dissolved." In only six years, Adefa's relentless efforts had succeeded in purging countless Jews from all facets of clothing and textile manufacture, one of the nation's most important economic sectors. Through a combination of massive pressure, hateful propaganda, direct intervention, blacklists, sanctions, boycotts, and firings, as well as illegal takeovers, buy-outs, and liquidations, the German fashion world was *judenrein*, free of Jews.

Many of the Jews forced out of the fashion industry were deported to ghettos, once mass deportations began in October 1941. There, they worked endless hours under abhorrent conditions to produce clothing and shoes for Nazi officials and their wives, for the military, or for German businesses, which contracted cheap ghetto labor for huge profits. At one time described as too despicable, too degenerate to create fashions for the "noble German woman," ghettoized Jews were now feverishly sewing clothes for German consumers to wear. Other deportees were sent to the SS-run slave labor camps, where their design talents and tailoring skills kept them alive, but only for a short while. A select few were assigned to the tailoring workshop at Auschwitz, established at the urging of the wife of Rudolf Höss, the feared commandant of the death camp. While two female prisoners sewed solely for the commandant's family, some twenty inmates toiled in the workshop, where they produced extensive and stylish wardrobes for the wives of SS officers and the camp's female SS guards. Most of these prisoners, who designed and stitched and sewed for their lives, did not survive the genocide of the Third Reich.

Despite assurances to the contrary, the policy of Aryanization had a devastating effect on the nation's economy. Fashion exports dropped drastically, as did domestic sales. Consequently, unemployment in these sectors increased dramatically. The German fashion world, suddenly devoid of its creative mainstays, suffered irreparable damage from the effects of breaking up what had been a tightly-knit business community. Fervent Nazis with little design talent or apparel-manufacturing experience were often the eager recipients of liquidated or aryanized clothing enterprises. Occasionally, so-called "friendly" Aryanizations were arranged, whereby Jewish owners would sign over their shops to Aryan co-workers in the hope that their businesses would continue after they had emigrated to safety. However, those Jews whose firms were forcibly aryanized were coerced to sell at ridiculously reduced prices. Sometimes, they received no payment at all. The eradication of Jews from the clothing industry also had a tragic effect on German culture. The famous Jewish design and *Konfektion* houses, which had been instrumental in garnering international acclaim for Germany's fashion industry and had become deeply embedded in the nation's cultural history, were either closed or taken over by non-Jews and renamed. It was as though they had never existed.

ENDNOTES

1 All quotes, statistics, and paraphrases in this essay come from primary source materials. These include contemporary newspapers, journals, magazines, industry newsletters and reports, the papers of Adefa (the organization established to purge the Jews from the German fashion industry), and documents from the Ministry of the Economy, the *Sicherheitsdienst,* and the Propaganda Ministry. All translations contained herein are mine.

2 *Arbeitsgemeinschaft deutscher Fabrikanten der Bekleidungsindustrie.*

3 *Arbeitsgemeinschaft deutsch-arischer Fabrikanten der Bekleidungsindustrie* (Adefa).

4 The phrase was *"Ware aus arischer Hand."*

5 The slogan was *"Wir können es besser!"*

6 *Arbeitsgemeinschaft deutscher Unternehmen der Spinnstoff-, Bekleidungs-, und Lederwirtschaft* (Adebe).

7 *Lieferungs- und Wirtschaftsgenossen deutscher Mützenfabrikanten, e.V.* (Arwa).

8 The ordinance was titled *"Verordnung zur Ausschaltung der Juden aus dem deutschen Wirtschaftsleben."*

Der Chef
r Zivilverwaltung
n El...
u. Wirtschaftsabteilung
Bezirkswirtschaftsamt —

BWA Vb Nr. E   330421

Kleiderkarte

für Herrn _Thomas Josef_

Wohnort _Zell_

Wohnung _____

(Mit Tinte auszufüllen)

Die Karte gilt bis 31. August 1941; sie ist nicht übertragbar.
Die Karte darf nur zur Befriedigung des Bedarfs des Karten-
inhabers benutzt werden. Mißbräuchliche Benutzung wird bestraft.
Aus dem Zusammenhang der Karte gelöste Kartenteile und
Abschnitte sind ungültig.

Auf die Karte können die umstehend genannten Waren bezogen
werden. Bei jeder Ware ist angegeben, wieviel Abschnitte von
dem Verkäufer vor Aushändigung der Ware von der Karte
abgetrennt werden. Beim Bezug von Socken und Strümpfen
trennt der Verkäufer außerdem den entsprechenden Bezugs-
nachweis ab. Der Bezug von Socken und Strümpfen ist auf
4 Paare beschränkt. Davon sind 4 Paare gegen Entwertung der
vorgesehenen Abschnitte erhältlich. Zwei weitere Paar Socken
der Strümpfe können nur gegen die 1½fache Anzahl von Ab-
schnitten bezogen werden. Die Abschnitte I—VII sind für den
Bezug von Waren vorgesehen, die gegebenenfalls besonders be-
kanntgemacht werden.

Für bestimmte Stoffe und Fertigwaren sind Sonderregelungen
ergangen. Sie können in den Geschäften erfragt werden.

Beim Kauf solcher Waren, die mit mindestens 40 Punk-
ten bewertet sind, kann auf die schraffierten Abschnitte
auch vor der darauf vermerkten Fälligkeit vorgegriffen
werden. Das gleiche gilt für die zur Herstellung dieser
Waren benötigten Stoffe nebst Futter.

Ab 1. 12. 1940 darf beim Kauf eines Wintermantels
oder des dafür benötigten Stoffes nebst Futter außerdem auf die nicht schraffierten ab 1. 3. 1941 gültigen
Punkte vorgegriffen werden

Bewertung für Stoffe
soweit nicht eine Sonderregelung getroffen ist

A. Wollene oder wollhaltige Stoffe aller Art,
143 cm Fertigbreite = 16 Punkte,
je volle 9 cm größere oder geringere Breite
= 1 Punkt mehr oder weniger.

B. Kunstseidene oder kunstseidenhaltige Stoffe,
bis 68 cm Fertigbreite = 4 Punkte,
je angefangene 17 cm größere Breite
= 1 Punkt mehr.

C. Alle übrigen Stoffe,
80 cm Fertigbreite = 8 Punkte,
je volle 10 cm größere oder geringere Breite
= 1 Punkt mehr oder weniger.

Punktwert der Waren

Spalte I: Punktwert für Waren, die nicht nach II—I
unterschiedlich bewertet sind.

Spalte II: Punktwert für wollene oder wollhaltige
Waren.

Spalte III: Punktwert für kunstseidene oder kunstseidenhaltige Waren.

Spalte IV: Punktwert für Waren aus allen übrige
Spinnstoffen.

Fashion Disappears from Germany

Charlotte Schallié

Translated by Steven Taubeneck

The outbreak of the Second World War only slightly influenced the supply of goods in Germany, due to the victorious "lightning wars" *(Blitzkrieg)* and the economic exploitation of the conquered countries.

Rationing began on August 28, 1939, just four days before the war, with the introduction of the "Food Card" and a "Reich Clothing Card" that were distributed in November 1939. But overall consumer spending remained largely consistent from 1937 to 1942, and during this initial phase businesses were able to maintain a substantial selection of consumer goods. Inevitably, though, textile manufacturing was weakened by the war and by the forced transformation of important industries into armament producers. In particular, the smaller handicraft businesses of the middle class, for example, the tailors, dressmakers and shoemakers, were driven to layoffs and shutdowns. In addition, the lack of raw materials and the subsequent use of cheaper, locally-made synthetics led to obvious reductions in the quality of goods. One result was that manufacturers were no longer able to sew in the label claiming "Pure New Wool."

The Reich Clothing Card determined the number of clothing articles that a person could buy. It was valid for a year and

contained one hundred units, called "points," which were
used to purchase clothing with money. The clothing card set
the amounts and put clear limits on the selection of clothes.
In one year, women were allowed to have one pair of stockings
for 4 points, with two additional pairs if necessary for 8
points each, a scarf (5), a skirt (20), a suit (45), a summer coat
(35), a pullover (25), an apron (12), a petticoat (15),
nightdress (18), brassiere (40), corset (8), woolen knickers
(16), vest (10), dressing gown (25), a pair of overalls (25), a
woolen dress (40), a non-woolen dress (30), a jacket (25), and
a blouse (15). For men the selection included socks (5 points),
a pair of trousers (20), a vest (15), a shirt (20), a pair of
pajamas (30), a jacket (32), a whole suit (60), a raincoat (25),
a pair of shorts (12), and a scarf (7). All clothing that was
not absolutely necessary for everyday use – a fur coat, for
example, or wedding and confirmation outfits – was excluded
from the Clothing Card. Early in the war, fur coats were
greatly in demand and acquired through the occupation of
Scandinavia. Later, however, they were collected by the
"Winter Aid Agency" and sent to the Russian Front. Bridal
veils ultimately landed in the Sahara, where they were used as
mosquito nets by the Africa Corps.

FACING PAGE: Clothing drive.
SOURCE: BPK

ABOVE: German wartime clothing ration
card (1943-1944).
SOURCE: C. Jahnke Collection

PREVIOUS SPREAD: German wartime clothing
ration card.
SOURCE: Peter Mookg Collection

As the war dragged on, additional clothing cards became
available for adolescents, as well as ration coupons for winter
and occupational clothing, shoes, curtains, and bed and table
linens. But these coupons had first to be requested from
business offices and were granted only in proven cases of
emergency. In practice, this meant that they were almost never
given except if the applicant wore a gold Party insignia or had
corresponding connections. As of March 1, 1943, "Special
Ration Coupons for the Air Raid Wounded" went into effect.
These were intended for all those German citizens who had
lost their clothes and housing in air attacks. For the poor –
only if they were deemed "racially valuable" and "genetically
healthy"[1] – the National Socialist "Winter Aid Agency"
("*Winterhilfswerk*," WHW), also called "Winter Aid," had
begun to collect money, food and clothing in the winter
months of 1933-34, often using massive pressure tactics. Yet
by the second year of the war, Jews were refused Clothing
Cards by an order of the Reich Finance Minister.[2] Moreover,
the Jewish population had to do entirely without such food-
stuffs as white bread, fruits, sweets, cigarettes, and even meat
and fish.[3] In January 1942 Jews were ordered to give up all of
their warm clothing (furs, wool coats, and ski outfits). This
order was made harsher in the following summer when Jews

"Jews are to surrender to the authorities all fur items still in Jewish possession, including the smallest fur articles as well as collars and trimmings, even if the article of clothing is made unwearable by removal of the fur... We expect members to check their closets and wardrobes carefully to make sure not even the smallest fur articles remain. Non-compliance will be punished by the *severest measures* by the state police."

Nuremberg Jewish *Gemeinde* (Community), 1942

were also forced to give up all of their suits, blouses, skirts, hats, and undergarments as well as all fabric and wool remnants, and even had to remove the yellow "Jewish star" carefully so as not to leave a trace.

After the capitulation of the Sixth German Army at Stalingrad in the winter of 1942-43 and Joseph Goebbels' proclamation of "total war" on February 18, 1943, the Nazis rapidly turned larger businesses towards armament production and closed the smaller, less vital ones. From then on all production and distribution of goods in the Third Reich was directed towards the campaign. Even the display areas of the fashion houses were emptied of all but the naked mannequins. Whoever was still interested in fashion accessories had to acquire them through the soldiers at the front in the occupied territories. The field packs from France were especially popular, since they often included fashions no longer available in Germany. If a soldier on leave illegally brought home army goods to Germany, for example, the silken material from parachutes, this was promptly reworked into a fancy silk blouse or an elegant wedding dress. The approach was a kind of "improvised self-help," because the Clothing Cards themselves, which in any case were less available after 1942, had scarcely any more buying power.

	I	II	III	IV
Anzüge, dreiteilig (mit Weste)	80	—	—	—
Sakkos, Janker, gefüttert	42	—	—	—
Sakkos, Janker, halbgefüttert	39	—	—	—
Janker, Jacken (Sommertrachtenjacken, Leinen-, Wasch-, Sommerzwirn- und Lüsterjoppen, Sommer-Lodenjoppen und -Jacken), ungefüttert	—	28	17	25
Hosen	28	—	—	—
Stoffwesten	10	—	—	—
Pullover mit Ärmeln	21	—	—	—
Pullover ohne Ärmel	16	—	—	—
Strickwesten mit Ärmeln	28	—	—	—
Strickwesten ohne Ärmel	21	—	—	—
Berufsjacken, gewirkt oder gestrickt	44	—	—	—
Windjacken und Windblusen	25	—	—	—
Gummimäntel, Gummiumhänge, Mäntel und Umhänge aus Öltuch u. ä.	25	—	—	—
Popelinemäntel, ungefüttert	35	—	—	—
Lodenmäntel, Lodenkotzen u. -pelerinen	56	—	—	—
Winterjoppen, Lodenjoppen	60	—	—	—
Wintermäntel	120	—	—	—
Sonstige Mäntel	65	—	—	—
Arbeitsschürzen	—	—	5	8
Schals, Vierecktücher	—	6	4	4
Handschuhe und Fäustlinge aus Spinnstoffen, gewirkt mit Futter od. gestrickt	5	—	—	—
Krawatten, Querbinder und Schleifen	1	—	—	—
Arbeitshemden (ohne Kragen)	—	22	14	19
Taghemden (Oberhemden, sog. Sporthemden, Hemden mit Halsbund), auch mit einem zugehörigen Kragen	—	24	15	20
Polo- u. Charmeusehemden, m. lg. Ärmel	—	—	12	15
Polo- u. Charmeusehemden m. k. Ärmel	11	—	—	—

	I	II	III	IV
Polo- u. Charmeusejacken (m. kurz. Ärmel)	9	—	—	—
Nachthemden	—	—	19	30
Schlafanzüge	—	—	29	45
Unterhemden (ohne Halsbund), Unterjacken, mit Ärmeln	—	14	11	14
Netzunterhemden und Netzunterjacken	—	7	6	7
Unterhosen, lang und ¾-lang	—	14	11	14
Unterhosen, kurz	—	10	8	10
Netzunterhosen, kurz	—	7	6	7
Hemdhosen	—	14	11	14
Netzhemdhosen	—	11	9	11
Kragen	1	—	—	—
Socken, gestrickt	6	—	—	—
Socken, gewirkt	4	—	—	—
Strümpfe, gestrickt, Sportstrümpfe und Sportstutzen	8	—	—	—
Strümpfe, gewirkt	5	—	—	—
Turnhemden jeder Art, Grubenhemden und -jacken	—	—	5	6
Turn- und Sporthosen	—	—	5	8
Badehosen, auch Dreieckhosen	—	9	6	6
Badeanzüge	—	15	12	15
Bademäntel	30	—	—	—
Trainingsanzüge	—	—	30	38
Trainingshosen, Eislaufhosen	—	—	14	18
Trainingsjacken	—	—	16	20
Taschentücher	1	—	—	—
Strick- und Handarbeitsgarne 100 g	4 bis 6			

Weitere Waren sind aus einem Katalog zu ersehen, der zu dieser Kleiderkarte herausgegeben wurde und bei allen Einzelhändlern eingesehen werden kann.

Zum Beispiel:

	I	II	III	IV
Ersatzmanschetten (Paar)	—	—	2	2
Kurze Trachtenhosen	21	—	—	—

c	d	e	f
Bezugsnachweis über 1 Paar Strümpfe oder Socken, zu beziehen ab 1.3. 41	Bezugsnachweis über 1 Paar Strümpfe oder Socken, zu beziehen ab 1.5. 41	Bezugsnachweis über 1 weiteres Paar Strümpfe ob. Socken, zu beziehen ab 1.10. 40	Bezugsnachweis über 1 weiteres Paar Strümpfe ob. Socken, zu beziehen ab 1. 6. 41

ABOVE: German wartime clothing ration card.
SOURCE: Peter Mookg Collection

With the establishment of official trade centers the German population had the chance to trade clothes, shoes, books, and household items for other consumer goods. In his diary entry of February 8, 1943, Hans Georg von Studnitz wrote: "the lack of the most necessary items has become so great that even the simplest things can only be found on the black market or by bartering."[4] The idea that "necessity is the mother of invention" can also be seen in the stories of women foraging through their attics and basements and reusing the clothes that had become unfashionable since the Bismarck era: tube pants, chokers, and top hats. Because people could no longer afford to waste even the slightest object, everything was immediately recycled. In addition to parachute fabric, other sought-after materials were cloth sugar bags, rabbit fur, curtains, bedsheets (as diapers) and

"Brother National Socialist, did you know...that your Führer is an opposer of overdone dressiness amongst men and women—and fashion insanity, and that he is trying to achieve a return to simplicity and a reform of dress and that he expects you to join him in this battle?"

Frau Magda Göbbels and Frau Emmy Göring, wives of top Nazi officials, continued to buy from their favourite Jewish designers in Germany until official Aryanization in the late 1930s made it impossible. And while Hitler's mistress Eva Braun wore "wholesome" dirndls in public, she placed a last minute order for an elegant haute couture wedding dress (from designer Annemarie Heise, which she wore with Ferragamo shoes.)

sheep's wool. If their children needed new kneesocks, mothers reached for the wool that had been used to clean industrial machines and sewed socks from it. When these were cleaned in boiling water, they became snow white and looked like new. Mothers with many children and women with health problems could take their patchwork to the public sewing office of the People's Welfare Agency, where seamstresses would help them make clothes. Since most things had already been taken, there was scarcely enough fabric for an entire jacket or skirt, hence people often dressed arrayed with patches, like walking advertising columns. Despite the severe conditions they still felt it necessary to cover the holes in their clothes. In addition, the willing buyer could occasionally obtain something from the empty businesses under the table, as long as she had the requisite object to exchange. After the deportation of the Jews began, it often happened that neighbors would plunder their houses and apartments and take away anything not nailed down.

Clothing continued to be produced in Germany, both through the private sector and in the concentration camps. In 1941 the Nazis created the "Women Help to Win" campaign, which aimed to put more women as well as the many foreigners to work, particularly in the textile industry. Textile production

The 30,000 to 50,000 women inmates in Ravensbruck concentration camp were each issued one pair of striped overalls or a long shirt and wooden clogs. By 1943, socks and underwear were no longer provided.

was intended above all for export to Sweden, since it was a creditor nation and the most important source of iron ore, and therefore central to German steel production and armaments.[5] After December 1941, concentration camp inmates began to fabricate uniforms and civil clothing under the pressure of high work quotas in the weaving and dressmaking shops.[6] In the archive of the Ravensbrück memorial, there is a report by a Jewish woman on her work as a dressmaker:

> *You saw only pale women at the sewing machines, anxiously looking around. The nearer the angry supervisor, an SS man, came, the more nervous and uncertain the tortured people grew. The saying was: the quota! the quota! But once a quota was reached, it was immediately increased and finally reached by beatings.[7]*

The camp inmates not only produced new clothes, they also reused material that had already been worn. Thus, as in Auschwitz-Birkenau, there was a team of sorters who sorted the goods from the new arrivals–which were handed over immediately on arrival–in storehouse rooms called "Kanada." As Raul Hilberg wrote, the concentration camps worked "quickly and

"A person stepped off the train in the morning, in the evening his corpse was burned and his clothing packed for shipment to Gemany."

Raul Hilberg, Historian

efficiently: a person stepped out of the train in the morning, in the evening his corpse was burned and his clothing packed for shipment to Germany."[8] It was also common to shave off the hair of the women inmates and sell it for 50 cents a kilogram to German textile firms, who used it to make "horsehair lining."[9] The majority of all the personal effects taken from the Jews and other prisoners was sent to Germany. These things went to the inhabitants of bombed cities or to the "ethnic Germans" in outlying areas. Often the goods would be sold in factories at giveaway prices. Especially valuable objects like pieces of jewelry were exported abroad, in order to generate currency for the purchase of the necessary raw materials.[10] It is hard to conceive today of the number of personal goods that were confiscated. It is also hard to imagine some of the grotesque discoveries that occurred: at the liberation of Auschwitz-Birkenau the Allies uncovered not only a terrifying number of bodies but a mass grave of another kind: 348,820 men's suits, 836,525 women's garments, 38,000 men's shoes and 5,255 women's shoes.

ENDNOTES

1   Hilde Kammer and Elisabeth Bartsch,
    *Nationalsozialismus. Begriffe aus der Zeit der
    Gewaltherrschaft 1933-1945* (Reinbek bei
    Hamburg: Rowohlt Taschenbuch Verlag, 1992),
    241.

2   Christian Zentner, Friedemann Bedürftig, et al (ed.),
    Das grosse Lexikon des Dritten Reiches (München:
    Südwest Verlag, 1985), 478.

3   Avraham Barkai, *Das Wirtschaftssystem des
    Nationalsozialismus* (Frankfurt am Main: Fischer
    Taschenbuch Verlag, 1988), 219.

4   Quoted in Willi A. Boelcke, *Die Kosten von Hitlers
    Krieg* (Paderborn: Ferdinand Schöningh,1985), 135.

5   Wolfgang Michalka, *Nationalsozialistische
    Aussenpolitik* (Darmstadt: Wissenschaftliche
    Buchgesellschaft, 1978), 350.

6   Hermann Kaienburg (ed.), *Konzentrationslager und
    deutsche Wirtschaft 1939-1945* (Opladen: Leske +
    Budrich, 1996),19.

7   Ibid., 202.

8   Raul Hilberg, *Die Vernichtung der europäischen
    Juden,* Bd.2 (Frankfurt am Main: 1990), 927.

9   *Auschwitz—faschistisches Vernichtungslager*
    (Warszawa: Interpress 1978), 121. Horse hair was
    used as filling material for mattresses and cushions
    at this time.

10 Ibid., 121.

Ridding Vienna's Fashion and Textile Industry of Jews During the Nazi Period

Gloria Sultano

Translated from the German by Alistair Mackay

"Their businesses are simply taken away from them and they are given nothing in return."[1]

THE FASHION CENTRES OF VIENNA AND BERLIN

Berlin, particularly in the 1920s, enjoyed an excellent worldwide reputation and was, along with Paris, Europe's fashion centre. This was also the case in Vienna, though to a lesser extent, where the textile industry was generally not financially strong enough to have a presence abroad. The Berlin salons of Marbach, Hoherz, Hilda Romatzki, Schulze-Bibernell, Böhm and Horn were the prominent German fashion houses; in Vienna it was the fashion houses of Getrud Höchsmann, Jerlaine, and the Tailors Stone & Blyth salon that set the tone. Within a period of five years the Nazis destroyed this significant element of the economic and artistic tradition of Berlin. It took considerably less time to do the same in Vienna.

Dressmaking at that time was primarily the domain of Jews. Almost half the textile firms in Berlin belonged to Jews. According to the German Association of Medium and Large Businesses, Jewish ownership may have been closer to three quarters of all textile firms,[2] a condition that the Nazis used to legitimize the expulsion of Jews from the clothing industry. The Nazi military publication *Das Schwarze Korps* was always preoccupied with the fashion world. According to their publication at the time, international fashion was like "spiritual cocaine" (*geistiges Kokain*) that served only to dull the minds of German women. Jewish fashion houses and business people wanted, they said, to poison Germans and were a moral danger for any woman employed in that business.[3]

Already at the end of the 1920s Jewish clothing businesses were the object of anti-Semitic propaganda and acts of aggression. After Hitler seized power, the Nazis called for an "Aryans for Aryans" fashion movement. Ideology was supposed to determine the direction of fashion in "Greater Germany," but the Nazis made exceptions for themselves. At party receptions, just as before, luxury and Parisian chic prevailed. For example, Emmy Göring bought her wardrobe in Jewish fashion houses as long it was possible to do so. The famous old salons were required to close by 1938 at the latest, and many dressmaking houses such as Gerson, Manheimer, Israel and Strobach in Berlin as well as Herzmansky and Gerngross in Vienna were Aryanized.

THE BOYCOTT

At the beginning there were calls for boycotts. Nameplates identified "German" businesses, while Jewish firms were besmirched. In Berlin, Jewish firms were branded with the owner's surname painted in huge white Hebrew-style letters on the front of the shop. Problems arose in Vienna where there were many "persons of mixed-blood" who according to the Nuremberg Laws were not to be considered Jews. Until the end of 1938 only Aryan businesses could be identified in Vienna. On November 11, 1938, the day after Kristallnacht, the new boycott measures were announced:

> *The Chief of Police in Vienna ordered that one avoid camouflaging Jewish businesses and that by November 15, 1938, all Jewish commercial establishments in Vienna be marked in the following fashion: next to the name of the company, to the name of the owner, or otherwise to the description of the company, the same words are to appear in equally large letters in Hebrew.*[4]

The limitation and eventually the closing-off of supplies of goods followed, as well as the exclusion of Jews from press

LEFT: Label from man's ski suit Vienna, 1930's.
SOURCE: C. Jahnke Collection

FACING PAGE: Three Jewish businessmen are forced to march down Bruehl Strasse in central Leipzig in 1935. They carry signs that read: "Do not buy from Jews. Shop in German businesses!" One of those marching is Chaim Bleiweiss, owner of the Kaufhaus Bruehl department store. The photo was sold as a postcard in Leipzig.
SOURCE: USHMM Archives

LOWER RIGHT: Label from man's formal dress shirt, Vienna, c. 1930.
SOURCE: C. Jahnke Collection

notices and fashion shows. These restrictions were followed by illegal firings and the presence of spies and informers within Jewish businesses. These enforced business practices were called Aryanization. Even the good relationships typical in the fashion world between Jews and Aryans could neither prevent nor lessen these actions. By 1939 the business life of Jews was greatly handicapped and limited but the forced Aryanizations and numerous liquidations were yet to come. Jews were forced to emigrate; some went underground. Those who wanted to stay or had to remain were dragged away and murdered.

ARYANIZATION

After the Anschluss in the spring of 1938, Aryanizations began in Vienna. The days after the Anschluss were marked by "wild Aryanizations," the plundering of businesses and homes and the hounding of Jews. Open terror reigned in the streets:

> *Things are happening in Vienna which in disgust and offensiveness go beyond what even the Aryan population could have wished for, and which thus create the impression of uncertainty about one's legal rights. Our beloved Führer and his henchmen supposedly have no idea what is going on. To the sound of loud caterwauling,*

Jewish businesses are besmirched by dubious figures led on by street gangs and mobs. Harmless people who either from ignorance or thoughtlessness buy something in a Jewish shop are molested in the most vulgar fashion. Passersby who look Jewish are violently and to the accompaniment of public mockery forced to perform the most menial tasks and more. The police see all this and do nothing.[5]

In Vienna, they didn't "shilly-shally" for long. After Hitler's seizure of power Aryanizations were carried out more "generously," more consistently and more quickly than in Germany. The case of Donau-Strumpf, a prominent stocking and knitwear factory, serves as a good example of the extent of the profits to be made from Aryanization. In August 1939 the factory was acquired by the Aryan Franz Schimon for RM (Reichsmarks) 11,000. The same year Schimon sold it to Richard Steppischnigg for RM 70,000. By mid-1941 Steppischnigg was ready to part with it for at least RM 150,000.[6]

Expropriations quickly came under government economic policy regulations. "Legal Aryanizations" controlled from above were introduced. Josef Bürckel, Reich's Commissioner for the

Reunification of Austria with the German Reich and later
Gauleiter of Vienna, organized a review of all confiscations in
the summer of 1938 and officially declared: "Let it hereby be
known that in the future even more than previously the slightest
misconduct on the part of a Commissioner who has to act as a
Trustee will be treated with the harshest punishment."[7] On July
2, 1938, the newspaper Das Kleine Volksblatt published the new
regulations concerning "the nature of the true Commissioner"
under the headlines: "Gauleiter Bürckel Takes Vigorous Action.
Twelve Disloyal Trustees Sent to Dachau."[8] In comparison to
the outrages rampant at the time, this was a relatively small number.

CONSEQUENCES

Aryanization and the "emigration" of about 100,000 mostly
younger Jews, the "cleansing" of professions, the "weeding out"
process and the "rationalization" of business concerns along
with "social measures" were supposed to be the preconditions
for the creation of a "new favorable development in the area of
the entrepreneurial and working sectors."[9] But the new owners
could seldom carry on business in the old, tried and tested way.

Aryanized firm names were new and unknown in the industry.
The poor business climate, greed for profit, and lack of

professionalism on the part of the Aryan owners as well as the
absence of the personality, knowledge and skill of the former
owners led to financial difficulties. Additional losses were
incurred through the incalculable foreign assets lost to businesses
after their former owners were forced out. Expenses increased
because the Aryanized businesses were now more dependent on
bank credit and because the new owners were obliged to let
their firms be managed by employees. Before long strong
competition arose, particularly in the textile sector, from firms
newly set up abroad by Jews who had emigrated.

The boycott from abroad brought with it further economic
difficulties. This led repeatedly to bankruptcies and eventually
to a drop in export figures. In 1940-1941 export numbers rose
for a short time as a result of new markets opening in Belgium,
Holland and France following the occupation of these countries
by German troops as well as in Spain, which opened up as a new
sales area.[10] However, on the whole export figures during the
time of the Third Reich never even approached those seen
previously. Even after the war it was extremely difficult for the
textile centres in Berlin and Vienna, always ranked behind Paris,
to regain the reputation they had previously enjoyed, due in
part to the traditionally Jewish textile industry.

Along with individual Aryanizers, Aryan businesses were also beneficiaries of Aryanization. The liquidation of many businesses brought a significant decrease in competition.[11] Banks and industry approved of Aryan firms need for expansion; Nazi economic planners put their concepts into effect. Even the State profited from the conditions of Aryanization. By the end of 1940 the Office for Property Transfer and the *Kontrollbank* allocated approximately RM 137.5 million for purchasing and supporting the Aryanization of businesses (approximately RM 25 million went to support). The government acquired still more profits from the confiscation of Aryanized Jewish assets, from liquidation proceeds collected from blocked accounts, through exceptionally high taxes on wealth (e.g. the "Atonement" fine and the "Reich Emigration Tax"), and from the straightforward confiscation of these accounts. Altogether billions of Reichsmarks were collected and sent directly to finance the manufacture of armaments.[12]

THE EXAMPLE OF TAILORS STONE & BLYTH

The Viennese *haute couture* salon of Tailors Stone & Blyth was able, due to the skill of its manager Fred Adlmüller, to survive the turmoil of the war relatively unscathed. Ignaz Sass, of Galician origin, together with his wife Stefanie directed the

Facade of Stone & Blythe, tailors in the Esterhazy Palace, Kärntner Strasse, Vienna.
SOURCE: Amalthea Verlage, Publisher, Wien

company that they had acquired in the 1920s. In 1930 the young Bavarian Adlmüller applied for a job with them. He progressed quickly, first becoming a dressmaker and then a manager after the Sasses decided to emigrate to London in the winter of 1938-1939.

On July 15, 1938, Sass registered his firm Tailors Stone & Blyth, a "Fashion-wares and Men's and Women's Tailoring Concern" as well as a branch establishment with two outlets in Bad Gastein on the official form (Number 44215) entitled: "List of property held by Jews as of April 27, 1938." The stated value was RM 40,000. In addition, an insurance policy worth RM 1,719 and jewellry worth RM 1,070 were included.[13] At this time the business was already being managed by a certain Franz Keller, who as "Commissioner-manager" was the only one allowed to represent the company. As qualifications for this position he included in his resume six semesters of electrical engineering, training and expertise in commercial enterprises acquired in his father's firm, and his early membership in the Nazi Student Union (1931) and the SA Margarethen during the summer of 1934.[14] In August 1938 Sass put his business up for sale with the Office for Property Transfer.

At an Executive Committee Meeting of the Office for Property Transfer on November 24, 1938, the business was sold to the "only applicant, Dr. Schindelka from the film industry. Jew receives RM 5,000 – Aryan applicant pays RM 16,000 – he is not an expert."[15] The purchase price was deposited to an account held by Ignaz Sass at the *Kontrollbank* three days after the contract was approved by the Office for Property Transfer.[16] A letter stated: "Dr. Ignaz Sass can dispose freely of the assets in his account to cover costs of travel abroad and for payment of internal obligations."[17] Sass thus received an eighth of what he had estimated the value of his business to be in his official property and wealth declaration.

Tailors Stone & Blyth was one of the few Aryanized clothing manufacturers able to continue working throughout the war. "The businesses are doing as well as before…, Stone & Blyth, under the direction of the go-getter Herr Schindelka, organized in the Hotel Kaiserhof (Gastein) fashion shows whose Viennese chic astounds the ladies Schirach and Göring …"[18] Yet with the beginning of the war, working conditions even there became more difficult. There were scarcely any private customers; obtaining material was extremely complicated; fabrics could no longer be bought abroad but had to come from the German Reich. Nevertheless twice a year fashion shows were organized, first in the Viennese House of Fashion and then in their own salon.

Since materials were still available for film productions, Stone & Blyth took up designing film costumes. Many film and theatre stars, such as Margot Hielscher, Paula Wessely, Marika Rökk, and Zarah Leander, considered it very important to appear on stage wearing an ensemble from Stone & Blyth. Even in 1944-45 Adlmüller designed the costumes – a total of 1,750 – for the first Willi Forst colour film *Wiener Mädel.* The fabrics for the costumes had to be obtained from all parts of the Reich. What was left over Adlmüller used for his first major fashion show after the end of the war.

THE RESTITUTION PROCESS

Fred Adlmüller, who had directed the businesses throughout the whole of the war and who had been in charge of the salon's artistic direction, was appointed public manager after the war. From London Sass had his Viennese lawyer initiate an application for restitution. On July 13, 1948, the Commission for Restitution decreed: "that the company directed by the opponent to restitution, under the name of Stone & Blyth successor Dr. Heribert Schindelka, is to be restored by seizure to the applicant for restitution, in exactly the same scale and state in which the said company now exists along with the branches in Bad Gastein."[19]

In 1948 the salon was returned to Sass. On June 17, 1949, the Sasses returned to Vienna from their London exile and took up residence in their former dwelling in the First Ward.[20] Thus Sass was one of the very few Jews who survived the Third Reich, returned and received back his former property, though greatly diminished, like other companies that were almost completely ruined by the war.[21]

The "Aryanizer" Schindelka, who in addition to Stone & Blyth had Aryanized a tie factory in Vienna's Second Ward, raised repeated objections to the regular court orders, for example, against the confiscation of his property located in Austria. However, for a long time he chose not to return to Austria. He was taken prisoner of war by the Americans, and later lived in Munich and Hamburg. As late as 1980 he was reported to be living again in Vienna.

Aryanization and Compensation – these issues are still not settled today and frequently cause a great stir in Austria. The History Commission set up by the government, which started its work at the end of November 1998, is investigating a number of issues including how matters concerning Jewish property and Jewish "returnees" have been handled since the end of the war.

Not only businesses and banks will be caught in the Commission's crossfire; political parties and even the State enriched themselves during the postwar period in Austria. The Viennese contemporary historian, Gerhard Jagschitz, writes:

> *Until now only documentary fragments exist on the question of Aryanization during the Nazi period and restitutions after 1945. Now we have, however, the unique opportunity to shed light on the unpleasant historical truth concerning a dark chapter of our history.*[22]

ENDNOTES

1 Anonymous letter to Bürckel, 21.7.1938. Bürckel Materie, Karton 173. Österreichisches Staatsarchiv, Wien. Quoted in Gloria Sultano: *Wie geistiges Kokain..., Mode unterm Hakenkreuz.* Wien, 1995, p. 241.

2 cf. "Keesings Archiv der Gegenwart," Wien, 23.1.1938, p. 3393.

3 cf. *Das Schwarze Korps,* Newspaper of the SS (Schutzstaffel) of the National Socialist German Workers' Party (NSDAP), 4.8.1938 and 28.8.1938.

4 Keesings Archiv. 12.11.1938, p. 3805.

5 Anonymous letter to Bürckel, 27.4.1938. Bürckel Materie, Karton 173. Österreichisches Staatsarchiv, Wien.

6 cf. Letter from the Office for Property Transfer to the Reich's Leader, 5.6.1942. Reichsstatthalterei Wien, Karton 15, Österreichisches Staatsarchiv, Wien.

7 Announcement by Bürckel, 28.6.1938. Bürckel Materie, Karton 5/12. Österreichisches Staatsarchiv, Wien.

8 Herbert Rosenkranz. *Verfolgung und Selbstbehauptung, Die Juden in Österreich 1938-1945.* Wien, 1978. p. 67.

9 Friedl Ehrlich-Steiner: "Wirtschaft und Mode im Spiegel der Wiener Verhältnisse, Eine volkswirtschaftliche Untersuchung." Dissertation. Innsbruck, 1942, p. 123.

10 Germany exported primarily to the Nordic and Balkan countries, where exports just before the war were on the rise.

11 By 1938 the great majority of existing Jewish businesses (approx. 26,000) had been liquidated – only a little over 4,000 were allowed to continue operating. cf. Gertraud Fuchs: "Die Vermögensverkehrsstelle als Arisierungsbehörde jüdischer Betriebe." Dissertation. Wien, 1989, p. 205.

12 cf. Fuchs, "Vermögensverkehrsstelle," p. 208. Schubert mentions much higher figures ("Aryanization Costs" approx. RM 40.3 million). cf. Karl Schubert: *Die Entjudung der österreichischen Wirtschaft 1933-1945.* Wien, 1957, p. 125.

13 Official form: "Verzeichnis über das Vermögen von Juden nach dem Stand vom 27. April 1938." Nr. 44215, Vermögensverkehrsstelle VVSt. VA 44 215. ST 7807. Österreichisches Staatsarchiv, Wien.

14 SA = Stormtroopers, uniformed and armed political Combat Corps of the National Socialist German Workers' Party (NSDAP).

15 Minutes of the Executive Committee Meeting of November 24, 1938. VVSt. VA 44215, ST 7807. Österreichisches Staatsarchiv, Wien.

16 *The Kontrollbank,* the Ministry Responsible for Economy and Work, Reich's Commissioner Josef Bürckel, the Organization for Commercial Business, and other smaller Party committees together with the Office for Property Transfer took part in this Aryanization.

17 Notarized Record, 29.11.1938. VVSt. VA 44215, ST 7807. Österreichisches Staatsarchiv, Wien.

18 Herbert Schill/Fred Adlmüller: Der Schönheit zu Diensten, Wien/München, 1990, pp. 34 and 36.

19 Communication of the Government Ministry Responsible for Property Insurance and Economic Planning, 27.6.1948. Handelsgericht. Wien. Hauptband "Stone & Blyth Nchf. Dr. Heribert Schindelka KG."

20 Shortly thereafter Sass had the "W.F. Adlmüller Co. Ltd." registered in the Trade Registry. Together with Adlmüller he directed the company. In 1950, Adlmüller took over the firm in return for payment in full of a Lifetime Annuity. cf. Hauptband "Stone & Blyth Nchf W.F. Adlmüller." 7HRB 28974a. Handelsgericht, Wien.

21 By 1953 approximately one quarter of the value of Aryanized businesses had been reimbursed. cf. "Mitteilung der Wiener Israelitischen Kultusgemeinde." 28.8.1968. Quoted from: Dietmar Walch: "Die jüdischen Bemühungen um die materielle Wiedergutmachung durch die Republik Österreich," Dissertation, Salzburg, 1969, p. 7. More recent statistics on the "Restitution Process" are outstanding. According to communication from

Brigitte Bailer-Galanda, Dokumentationsarchiv des österreichischen Widerstandes, 30.11.1998, the brochure of the Federal Press Service of 1988 "Measures taken by the Republic of Austria in favour of victims of persecution for specific political, religious or ethnic reasons since 1945" mentions 43,000 "affirmatively settled applications for restitution."

22 "Rückstellungen nach 54 Jahren, Eine Kommission soll entscheiden" in: Die Ganze Woche, No. 48/98, Wien, 11.11.1998, p.9.

CONTRIBUTORS

Christopher R. Friedrichs is Professor of History at the University of British Columbia, where he has taught since 1973. He is the author of three books: *Urban Society in an Age of War: Nördlingen, 1580-1720* (1979); *The Early Modern City, 1450-1750* (1995); and *Urban Politics in Early Modern Europe* (2005). In addition, he has published numerous articles on German urban history and on the history of Jews in Germany.

Irene Guenther is Assistant Professor of History at Marquette University. She received her Ph.D. in modern European history from the University of Texas. Her interests include war and women, comparative 20th century genocides, and modern European cultural history. She has published articles and essays on literary Magical Realism, Neue Sachlichkeit art, German émigré artists, cultural policies in Vichy France, and fascist fashion. Her book *Nazi "Chic"? Fashioning Women in the Third Reich* (2004) was awarded the Sierra Prize for best history book by a female historian (2005) and the Millia Davenport Award for best book on fashion or fashion history (2005).

Roberta Kremer is currently Executive Director of the Vancouver Holocaust Education Centre. She has curated numerous exhibitions, including *Faces of Loss* (2005) and *Ravensbrück: Forgotten Women of the Holocaust* (2003). Dr. Kremer received her Ph.D. in multicultural and museum education from the University of British Columbia in 1992. Her research has focused on collecting, historical memory and Holocaust literature. Dr. Kremer edited *Memory and Mastery* (2001), a full-length study of Primo Levi, Italian writer and Holocaust survivor.

Ingrid Loschek is Professor of History and Theory of Fashion at the University of Applied Arts and Sciences in Pforzheim, Germany. She has been a visiting professor at Harvard University and at Japan Women's University in Tokyo. Her current research is on women's emancipation from the 1850s to 1990s as communicated through fashion. Dr. Loschek has published numerous articles on social history and fashion including *Fashion of the Century. Chronik der Mode von 1900 bis heute* (2001) and *Reclams Mode- und Kostümlexikon* (2005).

Charlotte Schallié received her Ph.D. in Germanic Studies from the University of British Columbia in 2004. Her research interests include modern German, Austrian and Swiss writing, German Jewish literature after 1945, theories of cultural and collective memory, and representations of World War II and the Holocaust in literature. Her book *Heimdurchsuchungen: Deutschschweizer Literatur, Geschichtspolitik und Erinnerungskultur seit 1965* will be published in 2006.

Christian Schramm is an architect and city planner in Gelsenkirchen-Buer, Germany. His firm, Schramm Architekt & Stadtplaner, is involved in projects ranging from family housing to the large-scale planning of universities and municipal buildings. Dr. Schramm completed his professional studies at RWTH-Aachen University of Technology, where he received both his Diploma in Architecture (1984) and his Ph.D. in Engineering (1991).

Gloria Sultano is a cultural historian, journalist, and archivist. She received her Ph.D. in history and journalism from the University of Vienna in 1994. Her areas of research are contemporary history, oral history, history of daily life, and cultural history. Dr. Sultano is the author of *Wie geistiges Kokain, Mode untem Hakenkreuz* (1995) and co-author of *Oskar Kokoschka: Kunst und Politik 1937-1950* (2003).